Education and Sustainable Development in the Context of Crises

Education and Sustainable Development in the Context of Crises: International Case Studies of Transformational Change

EDITED BY

IRYNA KUSHNIR
Nottingham Trent University, UK

KRISHAN SOOD
Nottingham Trent University, UK

MIRIAM SANG-AH PARK
Nottingham Trent University, UK

HUA ZHONG
Nottingham Trent University, UK

AND

NATASHA SERRET
Nottingham Trent University, UK

United Kingdom – North America – Japan – India – Malaysia – China

Emerald Publishing Limited
Emerald Publishing, Floor 5, Northspring, 21-23 Wellington Street, Leeds LS1 4DL.

First edition 2025

Editorial matter and selection © 2025 Iryna Kushnir, Krishan Sood, Miriam Sang-Ah Park, Hua Zhong, and Natasha Serret. Individual chapters © 2025 the authors. Published by Emerald Publishing Limited. These works are published under the Creative Commons Attribution (CC BY 4.0) licence. Anyone may reproduce, distribute, translate and create derivative works of these works (for both commercial and non-commercial purposes), subject to full attribution to the original publication and authors. The full terms of this licence may be seen at http://creativecommons.org/licences/by/4.0/legalcode

Reprints and permissions service
Contact: www.copyright.com

No part of this book may be reproduced, stored in a retrieval system, transmitted in any form or by any means electronic, mechanical, photocopying, recording or otherwise without either the prior written permission of the publisher or a licence permitting restricted copying issued in the UK by The Copyright Licensing Agency and in the USA by The Copyright Clearance Center. Any opinions expressed in the chapters are those of the authors. Whilst Emerald makes every effort to ensure the quality and accuracy of its content, Emerald makes no representation implied or otherwise, as to the chapters' suitability and application and disclaims any warranties, express or implied, to their use.

British Library Cataloguing in Publication Data
A catalogue record for this book is available from the British Library

ISBN: 978-1-83797-776-5 (Print)
ISBN: 978-1-83797-773-4 (Online)
ISBN: 978-1-83797-775-8 (Epub)

INVESTOR IN PEOPLE

This book is dedicated to the people who live in war zones and suffer from the injustice inflicted upon them. Our thoughts are with them.

Contents

List of Tables and Figures — *ix*

List of Abbreviations and Acronyms — *xi*

About the Editors — *xiii*

About the Contributors — *xv*

Acknowledgements — *xix*

Part I

Chapter 1   Introduction
Iryna Kushnir — *3*

Chapter 2   Conceptualising the International Phenomenon of *Crises*
Iryna Kushnir and Nuve Yazgan — *9*

Part II

Chapter 3   Assessing the Social Impact of an American Liberal Arts University: Implications and Challenges in the Post-conflict Society of Iraqi Kurdistan
Hayfa Jafar and Munirah Eskander — *25*

Chapter 4   Leading The Policy Landscape of Somali Private Education System in a Conflict Zone: Views of Somali Headteachers
Krishan Sood and Abdishakur Tarah — *45*

Chapter 5   Towards a Sustainable and Balanced Development of Higher Education in South Korea
Sang-Seok Moon and Miriam Sang-Ah Park — *57*

Part III

Chapter 6 Migration in Education Research: A Synthesis to Support Sustainable Development
F. Sehkar Fayda-Kinik and Aylin Kirisci-Sarikaya　　　　*73*

Part IV

Chapter 7 The Potential of Teacher–Student Communicative Action to Overcome the Repercussions of Global Crises
Jennifer Swinehart　　　　*109*

Chapter 8 The Inner Development Goals: Changing Educational Systems to Meet the Challenge of Human–Generated Global Crises
Phil Wood　　　　*125*

Chapter 9 Conclusion
Miriam Sang-Ah Park　　　　*141*

Index　　　　*145*

List of Tables and Figures

Tables

Table 3.1.	Interviewee Themes and Onyx's Dimensions.	32
Table 3.2.	Overview of AUIS Organisational Affiliates and Programmes.	34
Table 6.1.	Inclusion and Exclusion Criteria.	80
Table 6.2.	Distribution of Micro-Level Citation Topics.	83
Table 6.3.	Distribution of Migration Studies in Education by Journal.	84
Table 6.4.	Number of Authors Contributing to Papers.	85
Table 6.5.	Most-Cited Migration Studies in Education.	86
Table 6.6.	Results of Keyword Examination.	88
Table 6.7.	Results of Co-authorship Analysis by Country.	90
Table 7.1.	Based on Key Aspects of the Education for Global Citizenship Sub-fields as Identified by Mannion et al. (2011).	111
Table 8.1.	The Elements of the IDGs.	133

Figures

Fig. 6.1.	Research Model.	79
Fig. 6.2.	Eligible Publications.	81
Fig. 6.3.	Distribution of Publications with Citations Per Year.	82
Fig. 6.4.	Mapping Results of Keywords.	88
Fig. 6.5.	Collaborative Relationships Across Countries.	91
Fig. 6.6.	Connection Map of Interrelated Migration Studies in Education.	92
Fig. 6.7.	Results of Cluster Analysis.	93
Fig. 8.1.	The SDGs.	129
Fig. 8.2.	The role of Education in Bringing Together the Micro-scale (IDGs) and the Macro-scale (SDGs).	135

List of Abbreviations and Acronyms

AEIC	AUIS Entrepreneurship and Innovation Centre
APP	Academic Preparatory Programme
AUIS	American University of Iraq, Sulaimani
CACHE	AUIS Center for Archaeology and Cultural Heritage
CGDS	The Center for Gender and Development Studies
ESDC	Education for Sustainable Development Committee
ESG	Environment, Society and Governance
ESSP	Education Sector Strategic Plan
IRIS	AUIS Institute of Regional and International Studies
ISS	International Social Science
K-SDGs	Korean Sustainable Development Goals
MOECHE	Ministry of Education, Culture and Higher Education
NGO	Non-governmental Organisation
OECD	Organisation for Economic Co-operation and Development
P3L	Place, Problem, and Project
SCQF	Scottish Credit & Qualification Framework
SDG	Sustainable Development Goals
SCL	Student-Centred Learning
UNAI KOREA	United Nations Academic Impact Korea
UNDP	United Nations Development Programme
UNEP	United Nations Environment Programme
UNESCO	United Nations Educational, Scientific and Cultural Organization
USA	United States of America
WOS	Web of Science

About the Editors

Iryna Kushnir is an Associate Professor at the Nottingham Institute of Education at Nottingham Trent University. Prior to this, she held academic posts at the University of Edinburgh and the University of Sheffield. Her interdisciplinary research combines the following main areas: higher education policy and sociology, European integration and social justice. She is particularly interested, and has published widely, in the area of the higher education policy and politics of the European higher education area. Her interdisciplinary approach has led to empirical and theoretical contributions, which reveal how education policy, on one hand, and Europeanisation processes, on the other hand, are interrelated and mutually shape one another. A wider societal impact of her work is in co-establishing and co-developing the Ukrainian Education Research Association which has become the biggest national research association in Ukraine and a hub for education research and quality.

Krishan Sood is a Senior Lecturer at the Nottingham Institute of Education at Nottingham Trent University (NTU). He has held course leadership roles at NTU on MA Education and the Foundation Degree in Education Policy and Practice since joining NTU. He has leadership and management experience gained across different education sectors, industry and leadership. He started as a Science Teacher in Derbyshire secondary school. He has taught in four universities in England. Currently, he is the Course Leader for Foundation Degree in Education Policy and Practice at NTU. His expertise is in educational leadership for diversity, social justice and inclusion. His research interests and publications are in the areas of leadership and diversity management, English as additional language, gender, early years and leadership, initial teacher training and teaching and learning and has published nationally and internationally. A wider societal impact of his work is in fostering international partnerships with global universities like University of Pretoria and Jyvaskyla, Finland, on researching early years/early childhood education that promotes equity among teachers, leaders, academics, students, parents and the wider community.

Miriam Sang-Ah Park is a Principal Lecturer (Internationalisation and External Partnership) at the School of Social Sciences at Nottingham Trent University, and a major part of her job entails connecting globally with higher education institutions across the world. She is also a research psychologist with a keen interest in topics such as psychological well-being and resilience across generations and works closely with researchers from different disciplines on related topics. She has taught classes on cultural and cross-cultural psychology, positive psychology and social psychology. She has served as Associate and Invited Editors for journals such as the *British Journal of Social Psychology* and *Frontiers in Psychology*. She obtained her PhD in Cross-cultural Psychology from Brunel University, UK, and has an international profile. Many of her collaborators are from outside of the United Kingdom, and one of the core areas of her research has been international and decolonial education as her publication record demonstrates.

Hua Zhong is an Associate Professor and Module Leader specialising in building engineering services, sustainable technology and digital construction. With over 20 years of professional experience, her research and teaching interests include low-carbon design, building performance simulation, intelligent buildings and sustainability in the built environment. She has published extensively in her field, with over 30 peer-reviewed journal papers and books chapters. She has generated over £500,000 in research and consultancy income, leading projects for organisations such as the British Council, NERC and the National Trust. Her consultancy experience includes major infrastructure projects like Crossrail, Beijing National Stadium and McArthurGlen Designer Outlets. She provides leadership through committees and boards like the CIBSE Regional Committee, Women in Engineering Society and the American Society of Heating, Refrigerating and Air-Conditioning Engineers. She holds qualifications such as Chartered Engineer, Fellow of CIBSE and Senior Fellow of the Higher Education Academy.

Natasha Serret is a Senior Lecturer and Senior Fellow at the Nottingham Institute of Education at Nottingham Trent University. Previously, she held academic posts at King's College, London, as a post-doc researcher and senior research officer, working on several large international and national research projects. At the start of her career, she was a primary classroom teacher. Her scholarly research expertise focusses on enabling the pedagogical transformation of classroom teachers in assessment and cognition in science. Pedagogical transformation is embodied in her research in Assessment for Learning and Cognitive Acceleration through Science Education. Her recognised authority in primary science is evident in her long-standing active membership with the National Association for Science Education (ASE). Over the course of 25 years, she has been appointed to a number of roles including Co-chair of the International Committee (2022) and Co-editor of the ASE Guide to Primary Science Education (2018). She is currently the Editor for the ASE Science Teacher Education online hub. Across this work, she has forged purposeful engagement between classroom practice and educational research nationally and internationally. She serves to support communities of science practitioners and uses over-arching themes, such as sustainability in science education, to ensure that a global perspective is maintained in science teachers' articulation and reflection of their practice. As recognition of her work, she was awarded the ASE Special Service award for her contribution to science education in 2018.

About the Contributors

Munirah Eskander is a Research Operations Associate with J-PAL Middle East and North Africa and the Sheikh Saud bin Saqr Al Qasimi Foundation for Policy Research. She is a former Adjunct Lecturer and Jan Warner Visiting Scholar at the American University of Iraq, Sulaimani, teaching in the English and Social Sciences departments. She is also a Research Fellow with Women Living Under Muslim Laws, a transnational feminist solidarity network based in the United Kingdom. She holds a master's degree in Modern Middle Eastern Studies from Leiden University in the Netherlands, as well as a dual bachelor's degree in Chemical Engineering and International Studies from the American University of Sharjah in the United Arab Emirates. A recipient of the Mahmoud S. Rabbani Scholarship from the Lutfia Rabbani Foundation, her research focusses on the Gulf specifically, especially Saudi Arabia, and the Middle East and North Africa more broadly, including Iraqi-Kurdistan. Her interests include gender and sexuality, political and Islamic reform, social justice, the intersection between language learning and critical thinking and educational developments in the Arab world.

F. Sehkar Fayda-Kinik is currently a Senior Lecturer at Istanbul Technical University, Turkey. After gaining her master's degree in Educational Administration and Supervision, she started to work for Istanbul Technical University as a Lecturer embracing teaching undergraduate students and research. Before embarking on an academic career, she received her PhD degree in Educational Administration and Supervision. Her research has embraced educational sciences with a special emphasis on higher education, knowledge management, professional development, technology in education, leadership, comparative education and sustainable development. She has been involved in a number of international projects on education. She is currently a member of the International Study Association on Teachers and Teaching, the British Educational Leadership, Management and Administration Society and the International Academic Forum.

Hayfa Jafar is a distinguished Institutional Effectiveness and Institutional Research Analyst, currently serving as the Manager of Institutional Research at Georgian College in Ontario, Canada. She previously held the position of Director of Institutional Effectiveness at the American University of Iraq - Sulaimani and worked as an Institutional Research Analyst at Centennial College in Canada. Dr. Jafar excels in both quantitative and qualitative research methods, having led numerous projects focused on measuring student retention and graduate outcomes, examining student social and academic experiences, crafting and overseeing strategic plans, establishing course review processes, and conducting preliminary research for new program development. Her doctoral dissertation explores the rationales behind the internationalization of higher education and the establishment of imported universities in post-2003 Iraq. Her research interests are broad, encompassing internationalization of higher education, international student mobility, international graduate outcomes and experiences, and the measurement of universities' social impact.

Aylin Kirisci-Sarikaya is an Assistant Professor at the Faculty of Education in Izmir Democracy University, Turkey. She has been teaching undergraduate and graduate educational sciences as well as educational administration courses. Prior to her career as an Assistant Professor, she taught in lower- and upper-secondary schools affiliated with the Ministry of National Education. She earned a master's degree in Educational Administration and Supervision and completed her PhD in the same field. Her areas of research interest include educational administration, educational policy, professional development, higher education, comparative education and sustainable development. She has managed several international projects, including EU Erasmus+ projects on teachers' professional development and growth, by engaging in international collaborations on teaching and knowledge transfer. Currently, she is a member of the Association of Educational Administrators and Experts.

Sang-Seok Moon is an Assistant Professor at the School of Social Sciences at Kangwon National University. He majored in historical sociology at the Department of Sociology at Yonsei University and in development theory at the Department of Sociology at the University of Texas at Austin. He is interested in the identity of the people who make up the society and the making of citizens who will be the subjects of the future society from Kookmin (National Subjects) formed during the dictatorship years of the past in South Korea. His current research projects focus on ways to invite and increase social participation from different age groups, including the youth as well as the older adults who make up a larger proportion of the population than before. He has published sole-authored and edited books including *Vestiges of Park Chung-hee's Mobilization System and the Formation of Modern Civil Society in Korea*.

Jennifer Swinehart is the Deputy Head of School at American School of Bombay, an international school in Mumbai, India. In this role, she works with staff, students and parents to help guide strategic educational and operational priorities in alignment with the school mission. She believes that all students should be empowered to pursue their passions as inquirers, collaborators and innovators to grow into self-directed learners. In over 20 years of experience in K-12 public and international schools, she has held various instructional and leadership roles through which she has advocated for expanding diverse and inclusive learning environments. In addition to providing a wide range of professional development experiences within her school community, she is a Principals' Training Center facilitator and Adaptive Schools Agency trainer and regularly creates and delivers workshops on coaching and adaptive leadership. Her doctoral research used Habermas' theory of communicative action as a lens through which to explore the influence of culture, society and person on students' learning lifeworlds.

Abdishakur Tarah is a Senior Lecturer and Researcher at the Nottingham Institute of Education, Nottingham Trent University, UK. He has extensive experience in educational management, and research areas in education in conflict and post-conflict context. His teaching practice focusses on special educational needs and disability, educational management and policy and social justice in education at undergraduate and postgraduate levels. He has a number of published works, including recent chapters, academic papers and educational resources in areas of action research, special educational needs, social justice and school leadership. He also served as Principal Advisor to FPENS, largest umbrella association of private schools in conflict-affected Somalia. He has worked as independent education consultant and worked with many basic and higher education (HE) institutions in Somalia as well as in other countries including Kenya, Uganda, Rwanda and Ethiopia. He is a member of global known education network and partnerships including Education in Crisis and Conflict Network and Higher Education Learning Network. His current initiatives are professionalisation of school principals in post-conflict Somalia and the role of HE institutions in post-conflict context.

Phil Wood is now a Professor of Education at the Nottingham Institute of Education. He began his career in education as a Geography and Geology Teacher in Lincolnshire secondary schools where he initially developed his interest in sustainability and environmental education. During this time, he was involved in national pilot curriculum projects before moving into teacher education at the University of Leicester. While leading teacher education and master's programmes, he developed a deep interest in how we understand and undertake change. Having spent five years at Bishop Grosseteste University, he was researcher development lead. Here, he continues to develop research into the nature of change, teaches on several undergraduate and postgraduate programmes and supervises a number of doctoral researchers.

Nuve Yazgan is a Research Consultant at Full Fact. She previously worked as a Researcher at Nottingham Trent University, Nottingham Institute of Education, and at University of Essex, Department of Government. She completed her PhD studies in December 2021 at University of Surrey, Department of Politics. Her research interests include European Public Policy, Greek Politics and Greek–Turkish Relations. She has previously published articles and book reviews in various journals.

Acknowledgements

We, the editors, would like to express our gratitude to all chapter authors in this book who have contributed their valuable chapters.

Part I

Chapter 1

Introduction

Iryna Kushnir

Nottingham Trent University, UK

Abstract

This opening chapter outlines the background and focus of this book and conceptualises our key terms, such as 'international development' and 'crises'. This chapter explains that by examining the relationship between education and international sustainable development in the context of crises, this book aims to provide a more comprehensive understanding of the role that education can play in international development and how international developments can shape education. The structure of this book is outlined as well at the end of the chapter.

Keywords: Education; international; sustainable development; crises; glocal; global

1.1 Background

This book aims to analyse the role that education plays in international development and how international developments shape education. This ambition is achieved through examining the relationship between education and international sustainable development in the under-explored context of crises.

Different traditions of sociological scholarly thought have appealed to the idea of an often mutually shaping relationship between education and societal development. A plethora of renowned thinkers from different temporal contexts

---

Education and Sustainable Development in the Context of Crises:
International Case Studies of Transformational Change, 3–7
Copyright © 2025 by Iryna Kushnir. Published by Emerald Publishing Limited. These works are published under the Creative Commons Attribution (CC BY 4.0) licence.
Anyone may reproduce, distribute, translate and create derivative works of these works (for both commercial and non-commercial purposes), subject to full attribution to the original publication and authors. The full terms of this licence may be seen at http://creativecommons.org/licences/by/4.0/legalcode
doi:10.1108/978-1-83797-773-420241001

around the globe have mentioned such a relationship. One example is Freire's (1970) powerful theorisation of the two scenarios of societal development and the role of education in this. In the first scenario, education is used to sustain an oppressive structure in which citizens are raised as passive recipients of the order that is imposed on them by the oppressors. In the second scenario, education serves as a liberating tool for bringing up critical thinkers who are enabled to seek ways to transform the society for the better. In both scenarios, there is a strong relationship between the nature of an education system and what happens in the wider society. In another example, Sen's seminal work on the Capability Approach highlights that human development and well-being could be measured and compared internationally only when considering the opportunities or, in other terms, freedoms that people have, and education should be one of such basic freedoms of every person (Walker & Unterhalter, 2007). The last example places an emphasis on education and the international, bringing us closer to the focus of this book.

Given the above theorisation of the role that education plays in international development and how international developments shape education makes it unsurprising that a number of theoretical and empirical studies on this topic have already been published. Their key foci include analysing internationalisation as a key contextual factor in developing education which, in result, is becoming more and more international (e.g., Cambridge & Thompson, 2004); discussing the role of education in the development of countries – for example, those below the top 50 in the annual publication of the United Nations Development Programme (UNDP) Human Development Report (Harber, 2014); problematising the relationship between education and national development as (not) always positive and present (e.g., Chabbott & Ramirez, 2000); and analysing education as a tool for fostering global citizenship, seen as a driver of positive change internationally (e.g., Mannion et al., 2016) and, more recently, also as a driver of international sustainable development (e.g., Jimenez et al., 2017). Education for sustainable development (ESD) has emerged as a 'buzzword' in recent relevant scholarship (Meland, 2022, p. 792). While ESD does uncover many nuances of the much-needed work that education can facilitate in achieving sustainable development, at the same time, it misses out on the focus on the role of contextual factors in the uneven sustainable development pattern around the world. Education may contribute to sustaining some of such disparities in the practices. Understanding and exploring the two-way relationship between education and international (sustainable) development, as explained more below, can help education institutions truly become vehicles of transformational change in the wider community.

1.2 The Focus of This Book

While all the above-cited sources are essential to provide an important account of the links between education and international development, they also evidence an apparent gap in our knowledge regarding this matter from a particular perspective of crises that have become an integral feature of global development. This broad gap is addressed in this book, while exploring the relationship between education and international development.

So, what does *international development* mean? It is a debated terrain. All the above-cited scholars have pointed out the evolving and complex nature of this concept. Harber (2014), for instance, acknowledges how pre-world-wars' vision of development that was associated with improvement altered predominantly after World War II (WWII). The world already clearly divided itself into industrialised countries and poorer countries, with the former being expected to help the latter in their economic progress. More recent 'social indicators' of development (e.g., health, education, well-being, environment) became more sophisticated, having 'put people at the centre' of development (Harber, 2014, p. 12). Our definition of *international development* in this book is informed by such a vision of international development focused on human development, albeit in the context of the aim of the sustainable development of our planet, as advocated in the recent Human Development Report 2021–2022 of the UNDP (2022). The report places the 'focus on the quality of relationships connecting people and planet' and also acknowledges the need to develop 'capacities to navigate uncertain futures', given the ever-emerging crises (UNDP, 2022, p. 60). In this book, we are concerned specifically with *international sustainable development*. The mere phrasing of this term to include the emphasis on sustainability aligns our discussion with the overarching aim of the United Nations' 'orchestration' of the sustainable development goals (SDGs) to resolve the issues that the planet is facing and improve lives globally (Kushnir & Nunes, 2022, p. 3). We pursue this alignment with the SDGs with the undeniable recognition of the crisis context in which international sustainable development has been facilitated.

Crises are complex interrelated phenomena, and sociologists have struggled for decades to arrive at a generally accepted explanation of what *crises* mean (Boin et al., 2020; McCormick, 1978). Nevertheless, all attempts in the recent decades to understand the phenomenon of crises with reference to international development, such as in McCormick (1978) and Boin et al. (2020), share the following commonalities: crises are a set of interrelated factors that disturb the normal operation of people, organisations, their relationships, resources, etc., and crises are integral to the process of change. The world has witnessed a plethora of various crises recently, including the development of post-truth politics, based on raising populism and fake news (Ylä-Anttila, 2018) such as in the phenomenon of 'Trumpism' in the United States (e.g., Miah, 2022). Other examples of crises include wars such as in Syria and Ukraine (Freire, 2022), persisting infringement on the rights of marginalised groups such as in the case of women under the Taliban rule in Afghanistan (Singh, 2022), climate change contributing to wildfires and droughts globally and even famine in east Africa (Warsame et al., 2022), as well as the Covid pandemic that has shaken the world on all fronts (e.g., economic) (Boin et al., 2020). The increasing 'glocalisation' – the interconnectedness between the global and the local contexts (Roudometof, 2016, p. 391) – indicates a (potential) growing interrelatedness between global and local crises.

There is, therefore, the need to explore the relationship between education and international sustainable development in the context of crises, which constitutes the focus of this book. Crises, such as economic crises, political crises, and natural disasters, can have a major impact on education systems and on the ability of education to contribute to development. By examining this relationship in the context of crises, this book aims to provide a more comprehensive understanding of the role that education can play in international development and how international developments can shape education. This understanding is crucial for those researching and teaching education and sustainability issues in higher education in order to inspire solutions and contribute to positive change in the face of crises.

This book presents a collection of analyses that explore various aspects of the relationship between education and international sustainable development, with a particular attention to various overlapping global and/or local recent or current crises.

The originality of the focus of this book is threefold. First, it locates the discussion of the interconnection between education and international sustainable development in the context that has not been the focus of related literature – the context of crises that are an integral feature of global development. Second, Part II of this book analyses three unique country case studies from a non-Western context (Iraq, Somalia, and South Korea), which showcase how the relationship between education and international sustainable development has been evolving in a range of different crises in these national contexts. The final part of this book proposes two unique avenues of moving towards addressing the world's interconnected crises through education in the ambition to facilitate international sustainable development.

1.3 Book Structure

Following this introductory chapter, this book develops in four parts. Part I includes a key theoretical Chapter 2 which conceptualises the international phenomenon of crises. Part II of this book comprises Chapters 3–5 which present three unique country case studies, namely Iraq, Somalia, and South Korea, on education and international sustainable development in times of crises. Part III includes Chapter 6 which discusses migration crises in relation to education as an illustration of the context of crises in the international domain. The final part of this book – Part IV – includes two chapters that discuss potential solutions to the world's crises through education. Chapter 7 focuses on the role of the 'communicative action' of the participants of the teaching and learning process, while Chapter 8 evokes the role of 'the individual' in the international sustainable development through pursuing the inner development goals. The final concluding Chapter 9 provides closure to the debates presented in this book.

References

Boin, A., Ekengren, M., & Rhinard, M. (2020). Hiding in plain sight: Conceptualizing the creeping crisis. *Risk, Hazards & Crisis in Public Policy*, *11*(2), 116–138. https://doi.org/10.1002/rhc3.12193

Cambridge, J., & Thompson, J. (2004). Internationalism and globalization as contexts for international education. *Compare: A Journal of Comparative and International Education*, *34*(2), 161–175. https://doi.org/10.1080/0305792042000213994

Chabbott, C., & Ramirez, F. O. (2000). Development and education. In M. T. Hallinan (Ed.), *Handbook of the sociology of education* (pp. 163–187). Springer. ISBN 978-0-387-36424-7.
Freire, M. R. (2022). Power and security in the mediterranean global south and at the eastern EU borders: Russia in Syria and Ukraine. In S. Panebianco (Ed.), *Border crises and human mobility in the mediterranean global south* (pp. 67–89). Palgrave Macmillan. ISBN 978-3-030-90295-7.
Freire, P. (1970). *Pedagogy of the oppressed* (M. B. Ramos, Trans.). Continuum.
Harber, C. (2014, May). Education and international development: Theory, practice and issues. Symposium Books Ltd. ISBN 978-1-873927-47-2.
Jimenez, J. D., Lerch, J., & Bromley, P. (2017). Education for global citizenship and sustainable development in social science textbooks. *European Journal of Education, 52*(4), 460–476. https://doi.org/10.1111/ejed.12240.
Kushnir, I., & Nunes, A. (2022). Education and the UN development goals projects (MDGs and SDGs): Definitions, links, operationalisations. *Journal of Research in International Education, 21*(1), 3–21. https://doi.org/10.1177/14752409221088942
Mannion, G., Biesta, G., Priestley, M., & Ross, H. (2016). The global dimension in education and education for global citizenship: Genealogy and critique. In V. D. O. Andreotti (Ed.), *The political economy of global citizenship education* (pp. 134–147). Routledge. ISBN 9781315540856.
McCormick, J. M. (1978). International crises: A note on definition. *Western Political Quarterly, 31*(3), 352–358. https://doi.org/10.1177/106591297803100305
Meland, A. T. (2022). Tracking education for sustainable development in ECEC institutions' annual plans. *European Early Childhood Education Research Journal, 30*(5), 791–805. https://doi.org/10.1080/1350293X.2021.2008464
Miah, M. (2022). Trumpism and racial oppression. In K. A. Young, M. Schwartz, & R. Lachmann (Eds.), *Trump and the deeper crisis* (political power and social theory) (Vol. 39, pp. 49–63). Emerald Publishing Limited. ISBN 978-1-80455-512-5.
Roudometof, V. (2016). Theorizing glocalization: Three interpretations1. *European Journal of Social Theory, 19*(3), 391–408. https://doi.org/10.1177/1368431015605443
Singh, R. K. R. (2022). Convulsed women's rights in Afghanistan pursuant to Taliban governance in early twenty-first century. In N. S. Manhas (Ed.), *Analysing the current Afghan context* (pp. 114–133). Routledge. ISBN 9781003365006.
UNDP. (2022). *Human development report 2021-2022*. Retrieved January 5, 2024, from https://hdr.undp.org/system/files/documents/global-report-document/hdr2021-22pdf_1.pdf
Walker, M., & Unterhalter, E. (2007). The capability approach: Its potential for work in education. In M. Walker & E. Unterhalter (Eds.), *Amartya Sen's capability approach and social justice in education* (pp. 1–18). Palgrave Macmillan. ISBN 978-0-230-60481-0.
Warsame, A. A., Sheik-Ali, I. A., Hassan, A. A., & Sarkodie, S. A. (2022). Extreme climatic effects hamper livestock production in Somalia. *Environmental Science and Pollution Research, 29*(27), 40755–40767. https://doi.org/10.1007/s11356-021-18114-w
Ylä-Anttila, T. (2018). Populist knowledge: 'Post-truth' repertoires of contesting epistemic authorities. *European Journal of Cultural and Political Sociology, 5*(4), 356–388. https://doi.org/10.1080/23254823.2017.1414620

Chapter 2

Conceptualising the International Phenomenon of *Crises*

Iryna Kushnir and Nuve Yazgan

Nottingham Trent University, UK

Abstract

Given that this book places the interconnectedness of international sustainable development and education particularly in times of crises at the centre of attention, it is impossible to disregard the nuanced nature of this crisis context. Based on a review of relevant literature, this chapter focuses on the following four main areas. First, it analyses the complex nature of the definition of the *crisis*, as multiple attempts to understand the phenomenon of crises and their various classifications have been consensual in recognising that crises are multidimensional and interrelated, that they are integral to the process of change and that they present a range of interconnected factors that distort the normal operation of people, organisations, their relationships, resources, etc. Second, this chapter explains the phenomenon of glocalisation in relation to crises to further detail how intertwined different crises are. When applied to the analysis of crises, the phenomenon of glocalisation is paramount in understanding how locally born crises can trigger globally reaching effects and vice versa. Third, this chapter discusses the impact of crises on international sustainable development. Finally, it is proposed in this chapter that education should be viewed as an important tool in tackling crises and, thus, easing the progress towards sustainable development internationally. This chapter provides

---

Education and Sustainable Development in the Context of Crises:
International Case Studies of Transformational Change, 9–21
Copyright © 2025 by Iryna Kushnir and Nuve Yazgan. Published by Emerald Publishing Limited. These works are published under the Creative Commons Attribution (CC BY 4.0) licence. Anyone may reproduce, distribute, translate and create derivative works of these works (for both commercial and non-commercial purposes), subject to full attribution to the original publication and authors. The full terms of this licence may be seen at http://creativecommons.org/licences/by/4.0/legalcode
doi:10.1108/978-1-83797-773-420241002

important contextualisation regarding the evolving multidimensional and intertwined crises against the background of which the discussion in this book embarks on in its subsequent parts.

Keywords: Crises; glocalisation; education; sustainable development; interconnection

2.1. Introduction

This chapter offers a valuable contextualisation for this book regarding the crises landscape. It is impossible to disregard the nuanced nature of the context of ever-evolving, interconnected and multidimensional crises, given that this book locates the intertwined nature of international sustainable development and education particularly in times of crises in the spotlight of inquiry.

The term *crisis* has been quite overused in recent years by scholars, political pundits and commentators. Several global/local events and developments have played a role in the growth of this crisis narrative. In the last decade, the world has faced unprecedented multidimensional and interconnected threats, including several economic crises, a few wars such as in Syria, Afghanistan, the Russian invasion of Ukraine, the Israel-Hamas war and resulting forced migration globally, more frequent climate change-related disasters, a steep rise of authoritarian regimes, the Covid-19 pandemic, to name just a few. All these events have posed a threat to the progress towards international sustainable development.

This chapter begins by a discussion of a definition of the crisis. It will then go on to explain the phenomenon of *glocalisation* (Robertson, 1992) in relation to crises to argue how interconnected different crises are. Then, it will examine recent major crises and how they have impacted on international sustainable development and education. Lastly, the remaining section of this chapter will discuss the role of education in international sustainable development in the context of crises.

2.2. Defining *Crises*

The definition of crises has been a controversial and much disputed subject within the field of crisis/disaster management and beyond (Aguirresarobe, 2022; Nabers, 2019). The terms *crisis*, *disaster* and *emergency* are used interchangeably in the literature although there are notable differences between them (Al-Dahash et al., 2016). Below definitions for each term will be discussed to present similarities and differences between them.

There are multiple typologies and definitions of crisis including *regular crises* (Rosenthal et al., 1989) and *creeping crises* (Boin et al., 2020, 2021). The regular crisis definition assumes that there is a crisis 'when political-administrative elites perceive a threat to the core values of a society and/or life-sustaining systems in that society that must be addressed urgently under conditions of deep uncertainty' (Rosenthal et al., 2001, p. 53). The key characteristic of this type of crises is that they are exceptional situations with a clear beginning and an end (Rosenthal et al., 1989). Another regular crisis definition is related to 'a sudden, negative, and temporally constrained change within a system which threatens to bring about a large and unforeseen transformation of a number of the identifying characteristics of that system and which urgently calls for new approaches and solutions' (Aguirresarobe, 2022, p. 17). An example of a regular crisis would be the Cuban missile crisis of 1962 that brought the world to the brink of a nuclear war due to a dangerous confrontation between the United States and the Soviet Union (Allison, 1969).

Creeping crises, however, have no clear beginning and ending (Boin et al., 2020, 2021). They can be undetected for a long time contrary to the regular crisis definition; creeping crises may provide a significant time for policy makers to address the potential threat before it escalates (Boin et al., 2020). One example of this is global warming and climate change. Defined by Boin et al. (2020, p. 3):

> A creeping crisis is a threat to widely shared societal values or life-sustaining systems that evolves over time and space, is foreshadowed by precursor events, subject to varying degrees of political and/or societal attention, and impartially or insufficiently addressed by authorities.

It is clear that both the regular and creeping crises definitions above refer to a threat to certain values and both are focused on the extent of management of the crises. This brings us to the need to juxtapose the terms *crises* as well as two other related terms *disasters* and *emergencies*.

There is no consensus among scholars on the relationship between the meanings of the terms *crises* and *disasters*. On the one hand, it is often the case that the terms crises and disasters are used interchangeably (Nabers, 2019; Shaluf et al., 2003; Wolbers et al., 2021). On the other hand, they can refer to a different nature of events (Boin & 't Hart, 2007). According to the second approach, disasters are sudden, short-term events although their consequences can last for months or even years. For instance, according to Boin and 't Hart (2007), the 2005 Hurricane Katrina and the 2011 Fukushima Earthquake are among the iconic disasters, whereas the Covid-19 pandemic can be better defined as a crisis as it may require a different analysis and solutions than the former one. Crises such as Covid-19 pandemic may not be framed as sudden events, instead an escalation process is part of their nature (Bergdahl & Nouri, 2021). According to some, disasters hinder state capacity which requires external assistance to cope with and recover (Coppola, 2015; Moe et al., 2007). Yet there may not be exact boundaries between the two phenomena – crises and disasters – as they are related (Shaluf et al., 2003). For example, the Covid-19 pandemic did require a lot of countries, particularly developing countries, to seek external assistance in, for instance, purchasing vaccines and supplying personal protective equipment (Chowdhury & Jomo, 2020).

Similarly, various perspectives exist on the meanings of the terms *crisis* and *emergency* and the links among them. Shen and Shaw (2004, p. 2110) put forward a definition that an emergency is a 'natural or man-made [people-made] situation that may result in substantial harm to the population or damage to property'. Alexander's (2005, p. 159) related definition of an emergency adds that it is

> an imminent or actual event that threatens people, property or the environment and which requires a co-ordinated and rapid response. Emergencies are usually unanticipated, at least in terms of exactly what happens and when and where they take place. However, they can, and should, be planned for.

A tsunami after an earthquake would be an example of an emergency event. However, a hurricane and an earthquake – classed above as disasters which are, arguably, a type of crises – can be also clustered as an emergency, and these can lead to disasters depending on how they are managed and averted (Shen & Shaw, 2004). Evidently, the boundaries among the terms *crisis*, *disaster* and *emergency* overlap and, thus, are blurred (Shen & Shaw, 2004).

Clearly, the boundaries between the terms *crises*, *emergencies* and *disasters* are blurred. A crisis may quite rightly be or turn into an emergency and a disaster. For instance, the 1962 Cuban missile crisis required agile decisions from the American and Soviet stakeholders that would have prevented a nuclear disaster (Allison, 1969). Therefore, if a crisis lacks management by the stakeholders, it may lead to a disaster (Davies & Walters, 1998).

According to various definitions explored above and illustrated by, for instance, Rosenthal et al. (1989), Boin et al. (2021) and Aguirresarobe (2022), the meaning of crises comes down to a major uncertainty, and it requires a reaction by stakeholders such as policymakers to seek solutions. The crises that will be discussed in this chapter and the rest of this book are not necessarily regular (fast-burning) crises. Instead, from the rise of populism/authoritarianism to climate change, these major threats are creeping (slow-burning) crises with no clear end and often leading to incremental policy responses (Boin et al., 2021). All of these crises are also interrelated which brings us to the idea of glocalisation which is discussed in the next section.

2.3. Glocalisation and *Crises*

The term *glocalisation* has made a scene in the scholarship in various disciplines including political science and sociology in the last decades. In his seminal studies, Robertson (1992, 1994, 2014, 2020) put forward an argument that globalisation is, in fact, *glocalisation*. This term refers to the simultaneous occurrence of globalisation and localisation trends in social, political and economic environments. Thus, glocalisation is about interconnectedness between the local and the global, the universal and the particular.

The origins of the term *glocalisation* derive from Japanese economists' global marketing strategies (Robertson, 1992, 1994, 2014, 2020). In other words, glocality can be defined as 'experiencing the global locally or through local lenses (which can include local power relations, geopolitical and geographical factors, cultural distinctiveness, and so on)' (Roudometof, 2016, p. 401). In this vein, Robertson critically debated the concept of globalisation arguing that globalisation, in fact, encourages diversification instead of standardisation (Giulianotti & Robertson, 2012). Several other scholars have also examined glocalisation (e.g., Bauman, 1998; Ritzer, 2003; Roudometof, 2016). While for Ritzer (2003, pp. 193–194), glocalisation is about local cultures' adaption of global features, for Bauman (1998, p. 70), glocalisation is associated with increasing global inequalities happening as a result of globalisation. Roudometof (2016, p. 403) defines glocalisation 'as the refraction of globalization through the local'. Therefore, global events have glocal dimensions (Roudometof, 2016). For instance, the reactions to the news of the 9/11 were divergent across different societies (Roudometof, 2016). Another example would be the management of the Covid-19 pandemic with varying types of policy solutions in different countries (You, 2020). With regard to these, glocalisation is also relevant for the crises literature considering how different crises hinder issues such as the international sustainable development.

The research to date has not focused on the interconnectedness of local and global crises. Understanding the link between local and global is crucial, considering the emerging issues of the last decades from climate crisis to economic crisis. A global crisis can have different consequences in different parts of the world. Climate change is a global crisis. Yet, it may trigger local issues in different ways. For instance, in the Asia-Pacific, climate change results in extreme events such as increasing floods and storms (Beirne et al., 2021). In East Africa, rising temperatures have caused severe droughts and famine (Devi, 2022). In Australia, rising temperatures are becoming an increasing threat to forests (Abram et al., 2022). These local consequences then will shape reactions and policies of the countries at the global level. In a similar vein, a local crisis can become global and shape the global responses by the international actors. For instance, Russia's invasion of Ukraine has triggered global reactions, illustrating how Russia is increasingly becoming a global threat.

Different types of crises (including disasters and emergencies) are a threat to human existence and the planet. Crises have an impact on all three integral and interrelated aspects of international sustainable development (Hummels & Argyrou, 2021) by, arguably, both hindering sustainable development and at the same time necessitating the search for solutions to the problems. Crises are likely to create additional economic, political and social vulnerabilities which will halt the process of positive change. For instance, South Asian countries like Bangladesh, Bhutan and Nepal are already facing major issues of poverty, health and education (Mall et al., 2019). An additional crisis is likely to further paralyse economic prosperity, environmental protection and human development. Less vulnerable, in other words, developed populations and regions are also subject to decline in terms of the elements of sustainable development. The multidimensional crises that the European Union (EU) have faced is illustrative of that. The European financial crisis, the populist/authoritarian pressure and others have revealed vulnerabilities of the EU and Europe that each led to damaging consequences of individual countries (Kushnir et al., 2020). Overall, we cannot separate international sustainable development from the recent glocal developments. The next section looks at these major events in more detail with a focus on education which has been emerging as a tool for sustainable development.

2.4. Recent Crises Around the World and Their Impact on Sustainable Development

The world order has been confronted with various crises in the recent decades. These multidimensional and interconnected crises have challenged the world's progress towards sustainable development, which is crucial to review before speculating about the role of education in solving these problems. Climate change, economic crises, authoritarianism, populism, wars and the Covid-19 pandemic, to name a few, have threatened human existence and its well-being as well as the planet. In the economic realm, for instance, several financial crises hit the United States in 2007, leading to the bankruptcy of the global financial services firm *Lehman Brothers* in 2008. This triggered the European debt crisis of 2009. EU policymakers responded to the crisis with the structural adjustment programmes which were implemented by countries like Greece, Ireland, Portugal and Spain (Parker & Tsarouhas, 2018). The European debt crisis has had social, economic and political consequences on the EU member countries as well as their nearby states and on the process of European integration. Citizens across the EU have lost trust in the European institutions and became dissatisfied with the EU, especially those who were hit hard by the crisis (Frieden, 2016; Roth et al., 2011). The economic crisis and subsequent structural adjustment programmes and the lack of further integration process increased opposition to the EU (Usherwood & Startin, 2013). The outbreak of the war in Syria led to a humanitarian crisis causing millions of people to take a refugee in neighbouring countries including Jordan and Turkey as well as to Europe (Stockemer et al., 2020). There has been a prominent surge of refugees coming to the EU borders during the post-2015 migrant crisis in Europe, putting a pressure on the countries of first entry, such as Greece and Italy (Landström & Ekengren, 2021). This was aggravated by thousands of refugees dying in the sea or going missing after arrival (Landström & Ekengren, 2021). Inhumane conditions of refugee camps often caught attention (Panebianco, 2022). Political debates have increasingly been shaped by populist narratives, making migration a priority in EU policymaking (Grande et al., 2019). The rise of populist and authoritarian forces has created a crisis of democracy and legitimacy not only in the EU but across the world. The 2016 BREXIT referendum was marked as the Eurosceptic victory (Usherwood, 2018). Populist voters around the world are found to be dissatisfied citizens who are unhappy about the workings of democracy. This can be observed in countries such as Brazil, France, Greece, Mexico and Turkey (Kaltwasser & Van Hauwaert, 2020). The Covid-19 pandemic came as a shock across the world, first identified in an outbreak in the Chinese city of Wuhan in December 2019. The pandemic caused various waves of public health measures across the world (Amin et al., 2022). Together with these, climate change vulnerability has been increasing day by day causing a threat to human existence in many forms, including droughts and famine in East Africa (Kemp et al., 2022). Crises are not limited to these developments. Many others, including the takeover of power by the Taliban in Afghanistan (Akbari & True, 2022) and the invasion of Ukraine by Russia (Kurapov et al., 2023), have posed a threat to democracy and legitimacy.

The above are only a few examples of the ever-emerging crises the world has recently been facing. Many crises are, arguably, interconnected, given the phenomenon of *glocalisation*, presented earlier. Many scholars have alluded to this idea, such as in the work of Pescaroli et al. (2018, p. 159) on 'cascading crises' and Losasso (2022, p. 7) on 'interconnected crises'. The crises discussed above are multidimensional, meaning that some of these crises have stemmed from the consequences of the others. Additionally, some crises have reinforced each other. In other words, there is no clear division between these different events emerging locally or globally. Some argue that the economic crisis and the so-called post-2015 migration crises in Europe played a significant role in the mobilisation of the populist parties across Europe (Taggart & Pirro, 2021). These threats have also affected the climate change crisis making countries more vulnerable to climate-related disasters due to political polarisation and dysfunctional resource allocation. The consequences of climate change are expected to continue reinforcing forced migration (Kaczan & Orgill-Meyer, 2020). Also, there is a link between far right/anti-democratic right and climate change (Forchtner & Lubarda, 2022). The Covid-19 pandemic has contributed into already existing problems the world had been facing. It started as a health crisis and then turned into a global economic crisis (Ozili & Arun, 2020).

2.5. The Role of Education in International Sustainable Development in the Ever-Existing Context of Crises

Quality education is one of the 17 United Nations' (UN) sustainable development goals (SDGs). Progress in improving education has been challenging especially in the regions with high social and political instabilities (Agbedahin, 2019). This is particularly problematic, given the role of education in reaching the SDGs (Becker, 2018; Merritt et al., 2018).

There can be various ways that crises negatively impact education and, consequently, restrict its potential in supporting international sustainable development. For instance, academic freedom has suffered in Turkish academia due to Erdogan's authoritarian regime in Turkey (Doğan & Selenica, 2022). Similarly, Hanson and Sokhey (2021) argued that higher education can be a tool for authoritarians to instil their ideas in the wider society, such as in the case of Kazakhstan. Economic crises and their consequences can place pressure on education across the world. Giroux (2015) argues that the rising cost of education leads to low-income and ethnic minority youth to be left out from schools. Wars have been one of the major stumbling blocks for both specifically education and sustainable development in general. One example is the gender apartheid in education under the Taliban rule in Afghanistan (Akbari & True, 2022). Climate change-related displacement will continue negatively affecting formal education and lives in general of the impacted populations, with over 140 million people being expected to be displaced in 2050, according to World Bank data (Rigaud et al., 2018).

As discussed in the above sections, crises have constituted threatening the progress towards international sustainable development. However, we could also pose a question about whether crises can be seen as an opportunity for policy changes towards sustainable development and whether education can be used as a tool in this process. Scholars argue that education can be used as a soft governing tool to attain other goals of international sustainable development (Kushnir & Nunes, 2022) such as gender equality, climate action, tackling poverty and others. Therefore, education can be a useful tool for reversing the negative consequences of the crises we have discussed previously. Focusing on education would help developing resilience towards potential crises and emergencies. Below are a couple of examples to illustrate ways in which education can overturn negative consequences of existing or future crises.

One important way is to focus on environmental education. It is significant to prepare societies to cope with climate-change disasters through education and learning (Hoffmann & Blecha, 2020). For instance, in regions that are vulnerable to extreme events such as fires, relevant information and resources can help societies to reverse negative impacts. Another example can be about focusing on green education practices worldwide to slow down and ultimately prevent the adverse effects of human behaviour on the environment, which threaten the existence of future generations. For instance, green university campuses have been implemented in Malaysia in the recent years, focusing on indicators such as food waste management, CO_2 emission management and others (Anthony, 2021).

Strong digital education is another illustrative way of education withstanding some crises and not compromising the learning of those involved. The transition to online teaching and learning that occurred during the pandemic as well as the invasion of Ukraine by Russia has shown that change can happen rapidly when needed, but it has also showcased weaknesses in resourcing and skills in many places around the world (Kurapov et al., 2023; Lennox et al., 2021). Indeed, such crises necessitate and enable changes in education systems to happen quicker than in normal times (Bojović et al., 2020; Langlois et al., 2020; Sá & Serpa, 2020). Evidently, such crises that necessitate education move off-campus present coping strategies for similar future events. They show that sector planning and budgeting needs to be more resilient (Lennox et al., 2021). Scholars recommend that educational stakeholders need to have sustainable and viable strategies to keep everything stable when crises emerge (Burgos et al., 2021).

Another way how education can aid international sustainable development is by serving as a tool for promoting democracy. Kushnir (2021, 2022) discusses this in a particular case of the role of the European Education Area in EU integration in the recent context of crises. These crises inspired the authors of the European Education Area to appeal to its education as an instrument specifically for EU deepening – one of the aspects of EU integration which is about the strengthening of the relationships among its member states. In particular, the European Education Area 'has been a driver in the development of a common European identity and European economy, the EU as a socially-just society and the continent of progress' (Kushnir, 2021, p. 301).

2.6. Conclusion

This chapter has provided a valuable contextualisation for this edited book regarding the ever-existing crises landscape. This book places the interconnectedness of international sustainable development and education particularly in times of crises at the centre of attention, thus making it impossible to disregard the nuanced nature of this crisis context.

Multiple attempts to understand the phenomenon of crises and their classification (e.g., Boin et al., 2020; İuyar, 2008) are consensual in recognising that crises are multidimensional and interconnected, they are integral to the process of change and they present a range of interconnected factors that distort the normal operation of people, organisations, resources, relationships among all of these, etc. The interconnectedness of crises is reinforced particularly by the increasingly developing links between the global and local context – in Robertson's (1992, 1994, 2014, 2020) terms *glocalisation*. When applied to the analysis of crises, the phenomenon of glocalisation is paramount in understanding how locally born crises can trigger globally reaching effects and vice versa.

A few examples of the crises that (different regions of) the world has been facing recently have been provided above and are further explicated in the rest of this book. What is crucial is that these major crises that we have faced have highlighted an important role of education in coping with these threats to humanity and the planet. Relying on education as a tool for development is key for coping with ongoing and potential crises, whether they are about democratic values or/and physical threat. In times of crises, education policies can foster change to adopt new realities. Societies can be made more resilient and flexible to these threats with the help of education.

References

Abram, N. J., Henley, B. J., Sen Gupta, A., Lippmann, T. J., Clarke, H., Dowdy, A. J., & Boer, M. M. (2021). Connections of climate change and variability to large and extreme forest fires in southeast Australia. *Communications Earth & Environment*, 2(1), 8. https://doi.org/10.1038/s43247-020-00065-8

Agbedahin, A. V. (2019). Sustainable development, education for sustainable development, and the 2030 agenda for sustainable development: Emergence, efficacy, eminence, and future. *Sustainable Development*, 27(4), 669–680. https://doi.org/10.1002/sd.1931

Aguirresarobe, A. H. (2022). Is national identity in crisis? An assessment of national imaginations in the early 2020s. *Studies in Ethnicity and Nationalism*, 22(1), 14–27. https://doi.org/10.1111/sena.12359

Akbari, F. & True, J. (2022). One year on from the Taliban takeover of Afghanistan: Re-instituting gender apartheid. *Australian Journal of International Affairs*, 76(6), 624–633. https://doi.org/10.1080/10357718.2022.2107172

Al-Dahash, H., Thayaparan, M., & Kulatunga, U. (2016, September 5–7). Understanding the terminologies: Disaster, crisis and emergency. In *32nd Annual ARCOM conference*, Manchester (pp. 1191–1200). https://openresearch.lsbu.ac.uk/item/872x5

Alexander, D. (2005). Towards the development of a standard in emergency planning. *Disaster Prevention and Management: An International Journal*, 14(2), 158–175. https://doi.org/10.1108/09653560510595164

Allison, G. T. (1969). Conceptual models and the Cuban missile crisis. *American Political Science Review*, *63*(3), 689–718. https://doi.org/10.2307/1954423

Amin, R., Sohrabi, M. R., Zali, A. R., & Hannani, K. (2022). Five consecutive epidemiological waves of COVID-19: A population-based cross-sectional study on characteristics, policies, and health outcome. *BMC Infectious Diseases*, *22*(1), 1–10. https://doi.org/10.1186/s12879-022-07909-y

Anthony, B., Jr. (2021). Green campus paradigms for sustainability attainment in higher education institutions–a comparative study. *Journal of Science and Technology Policy Management*, *12*(1), 117–148. https://doi.org/10.1108/JSTPM-02-2019-0008

Bauman, Z. (1998). *Globalization: The human consequences*. Polity. ISBN-10: 0745620132.

Becker, G. (2018). Climate change education for sustainable development in urban educational landscapes and learning cities. Experiences perspectives from Osnabrück. In U. M. Azeiteiro, M. Akerman, W. Leal Filho, A. F. F. Setti, & L. L. Brandli (Eds.), *Lifelong learning and education in healthy and sustainable cities* (pp. 439–469). Springer. https://doi.org/10.1007/978-3-319-69474-0_26

Beirne, J., Renzhi, N., & Volz, U. (2021). Bracing for the typhoon: Climate change and sovereign risk in Southeast Asia. *Sustainable Development*, *29*(3), 537–551. https://doi.org/10.1002/sd.2199

Bergdahl, N., & Nouri, J. (2021). Covid-19 and crisis-prompted distance education in Sweden. *Technology, Knowledge and Learning*, *26*(3), 443–459. https://doi.org/10.1007/s10758-020-09470-6

Boin, A., & 't Hart, P. (2007). The crisis approach. In H. Rodríguez, E. L. Quarantelli & R. R. Dynes (Eds.), *Handbook of disaster research* (pp. 42–54). Springer. https://doi.org/10.1007/978-0-387-32353-4

Boin, A., Ekengren, M. & Rhinard, M. (2020). Hiding in plain sight: Conceptualizing the creeping crisis. *Risk, Hazards & Crisis in Public Policy*, *11*(2), 116–138. https://doi.org/10.1002/rhc3.12193

Boin, A., Ekengren, M., & Rhinard, M. (2021). *Understanding the creeping crisis*. Springer Nature. https://doi.org/10.1002/rhc3.12193

Bojović, Ž., Bojović, P. D., Vujošević, D., & Šuh, J. (2020). Education in times of crisis: Rapid transition to distance learning. *Computer Applications in Engineering Education*, *28*(6), 1467–1489. https://doi.org/10.1002/cae.22318

Burgos, D., Tlili, A., & Tabacco, A. (2021). Education in a crisis context: Summary, insights and future. In *Radical solutions for education in a crisis context: COVID-19 as an opportunity for global learning* (pp. 3–10). Springer. https://doi.org/10.1007/978-981-15-7869-4

Chowdhury, A. Z., & Jomo, K. S. (2020). Responding to the COVID-19 pandemic in developing countries: Lessons from selected countries of the global south. *Development*, *63*, 162–171. https://doi.org/10.1016/C2014-0-00128-1

Coppola, D. P. (2015). *Introduction to international disaster management* (3rd ed.). Butterworth-Heinemann. https://doi.org/10.1016/C2014-0-00128-1

Davies, H., & Walters, M. (1998). Do all crises have to become disasters? Risk and risk mitigation. *Property Management*, *16*(1), 5–9.

Devi, S. (2022). Climate change driving east Africa towards famine. *The Lancet*, *400*(10347), 150–151. https://doi.org/10.1016/S0140-6736(22)01325-3

Doğan, S., & Selenica, E. (2022). Authoritarianism and academic freedom in neoliberal Turkey. *Globalisation, Societies and Education*, *20*(2), 163–177. https://doi.org/10.1080/14767724.2021.1899801

Forchtner, B., & Lubarda, B. (2022). Scepticisms and beyond? A comprehensive portrait of climate change communication by the far right in the European Parliament. *Environmental Politics*, *32*(1), 43–68. https://doi.org/10.1080/09644016.2022.2048556

Frieden, J. (2016). The crisis, the public, and the future of European integration. In F. Caselli, M. Centeno, & J. Tavares (Eds.), *The crisis, the public, and the future of European integration* (pp. 146–171). Oxford University Press.

Giroux, H. A. (2015). Democracy in crisis, the specter of authoritarianism, and the future of higher education. *Journal of Critical Scholarship on Higher Education and Student Affairs, 1*(1), 7. ISSN 2377-1291.

Giulianotti, R., & Robertson, R. (2012). Glocalization. In G. Ritzer (Ed.), *The Wiley-Blackwell encyclopedia of globalization* (pp. 25–42). Wiley.

Grande, E., Schwarzbözl, T., & Fatke, M. (2019). Politicizing immigration in Western Europe. *Journal of European Public Policy, 26*(10), 1444–1463. https://doi.org/10.1080/13501763.2018.1531909

Hanson, M., & Sokhey, S. W. (2021). Higher education as an authoritarian tool for regime survival: Evidence from Kazakhstan and around the world. *Problems of Post-Communism, 68*(3), 231–246. https://doi.org/10.1080/10758216.2020.1734839

Hoffmann, R., & Blecha, D. (2020). Education and disaster vulnerability in Southeast Asia: Evidence and policy implications. *Sustainability, 12*(4), 1401. https://doi.org/10.3390/su12041401

Hummels, H., & Argyrou, A. (2021). Planetary demands: Redefining sustainable development and sustainable entrepreneurship. *Journal of Cleaner Production, 278*, 123804. https://doi.org/10.1016/j.jclepro.2020.123804

İùyar, Ö. G. (2008). Definition and management of international crises. *Perceptions: Journal of International Affairs, 13*(3), 1–49.

Kaczan, D. J., & Orgill-Meyer, J. (2020). The impact of climate change on migration: A synthesis of recent empirical insights. *Climatic Change, 158*(3–4), 281–300. https://doi.org/10.1007/s10584-019-02560-0

Kaltwasser, C. R., & Van Hauwaert, S. M. (2020). The populist citizen: Empirical evidence from Europe and Latin America. *European Political Science Review, 12*(1), 1–18. https://doi.org/10.1017/S1755773919000262

Kemp, L., Xu, C., Depledge, J., Ebi, K. L., Gibbins, G., Kohler, T. A., & Lenton, T. M. (2022). Climate endgame: Exploring catastrophic climate change scenarios. *National Academy of Sciences, 119*(34), 1–9. https://doi.org/10.1073/pnas.2108146119

Kurapov, A., Pavlenko, V., Drozdov, A., Bezliudna, V., Reznik, A., & Isralowitz, R. (2023). Toward an understanding of the Russian-Ukrainian war impact on university students and personnel. *Journal of Loss and Trauma, 28*(2), 167–174. https://doi.org/10.1080/15325024.2022.2084838

Kushnir, I. (2021). The role of the European Education Area in European Union integration in times of crises. *European Review, 30*(3), 301–321. https://doi.org/10.1017/S1062798721000016

Kushnir, I. (2022). Referentiality mechanisms in EU education policy-making: The case of the European Education Area. *European Journal of Education, 57*(1), 128–141. https://doi.org/10.1111/ejed.12485

Kushnir, I., Kilkey, M., & Strumia, F. (2020). EU integration in the post 'migrant crisis' context: Learning new integration modes? *European Review, 28*(2), 306–324. https://doi.org/10.1017/S1062798719000425

Kushnir, I., & Nunes, A. (2022). Education and the UN development goals projects (MDGs and SDGs): Definitions, links, operationalisations. *Journal of Research in International Education, 21*(1), 3–21. https://doi.org/10.1177/14752409210889

Landström, Y., & Ekengren, M. (2021). Migration, Borders, and Society. In A. Boin, M. Ekengren, & M. Rhinard (Eds.), *Understanding the Creeping Crisis* (pp. 87–104). Springer International Publishing.

Langlois, S., Xyrichis, A., Daulton, B. J., Gilbert, J., Lackie, K., Lising, D., & Khalili, H. (2020). The COVID-19 crisis silver lining: Interprofessional education to guide future innovation. *Journal of Interprofessional Care, 34*(5), 587–592. https://doi.org/10.1080/13561820.2020.1800606

Lennox, J., Reuge, N., & Benavides, F. (2021). UNICEF's lessons learned from the education response to the COVID-19 crisis and reflections on the implications for education policy. *International Journal of Educational Development, 85*, 102429. https://doi.org/10.1016/j.ijedudev.2021.102429

Losasso, M., (2022). Interconnected crises and design complexity. *TECHNE-Journal of Technology for Architecture and Environment, 23*, 7–9. https://doi.org/10.36253/techne-12913

Mall, R. K., Srivastava, R. K., Banerjee, T., Mishra, O. P., Bhatt, D., & Sonkar, G. (2019). Disaster risk reduction including climate change adaptation over south Asia: Challenges and ways forward. *International Journal of Disaster Risk Science, 10*, 14–27. https://doi.org/10.1007/s13753-018-0210-9

Merritt, E., Hale, A., & Archambault, L. (2018). Changes in pre-service teachers' values, sense of agency, motivation and consumption practices: A case study of an education for sustainability course. *Sustainability, 11*(1), 155. https://doi.org/10.3390/su11010155

Moe, T. L., Gehbauer, F., Senitz, S., & Mueller, M. (2007). Balanced scorecard for natural disaster management projects. *Disaster Prevention and Management: An International Journal, 16*(5), 785–806. https://doi.org/10.1108/09653560710837073

Nabers, D. (2019). Discursive dislocation: Toward a poststructuralist theory of crisis in global politics. *New Political Science, 41*(2), 263–278. https://doi.org/10.1080/07393148.2019.1596684

Ozili, P., & Arun, T. (2020). *Spillover of COVID-19: Impact on the global economy*. SSRN Elsevier. https://doi.org/10.2139/ssrn.3562570

Panebianco, S. (Ed.). (2022). *Border crises and human mobility in the mediterranean global south*. Springer International Publishing. https://doi.org/10.1007/978-3-030-90295-7

Parker, O., & Tsarouhas, D. (Eds.). (2018). *Crisis in the Eurozone periphery: The political economies of Greece, Spain, Ireland and Portugal*. Springer. ISBN-10: 3319888307.

Pescaroli, G., Nones, M., Galbusera, L., & Alexander, D. (2018). Understanding and mitigating cascading crises in the global interconnected system. *International Journal of Disaster Risk Reduction, 30*, 159–163. https://doi.org/10.1016/j.ijdrr.2018.07.004

Rigaud, K. K., de Sherbinin, A., Jones, B., Bergmann, J., Clement, V., Ober, K., Schewe, J., Adamo, S., McCusker, B., Heuser, S., & Midgley, A. (2018). *Groundswell: Preparing for internal climate migration*. World Bank. https://library.au.int/groundswellpreparing-internal-climate-migration

Ritzer, G. (2003). Rethinking globalization: Glocalization/grobalization and something/nothing. *Sociological Theory, 21*, 193–209. https://doi.org/10.1111/1467-9558.00185

Robertson, R. (1992). *Globalization: Social theory and global culture*. Sage. ISBN: 9781446280447.

Robertson, R. (1994). Globalisation or glocalisation? *Journal of International Communication, 1*, 33–52. https://doi.org/10.1080/13216597.1994.9751780

Robertson, R. (2014). Situating glocalization: A relatively autobiographical intervention. In G. S. Drori, M. A. Hollerer, & P. Wagenbach (Eds.), *Global themes and local variations in organization and management: Perspectives on glocalization* (pp. 25–36). Routledge. ISBN: 9780415807685.

Robertson, R. (2020). The glocal turn. In I. Rossi (Ed.), *Challenges of globalization and prospects for an inter-civilizational world order* (pp. 25–38). Springer. https://doi.org/10.1007/978-3-030-44058-9_2

Rosenthal, U., Boin, A., & Comfort, L. K. (2001). *Managing crises: Threats, dilemmas, opportunities*. Charles C Thomas Publisher.

Rosenthal, U., Charles, M. T., & 't Hart, P. (1989). *Coping with crises*. Springfield. https://doi.org/10.1177/107554709101200402

Roth, F., Nowak-Lehmann, F. D., & Otter, T. (2011). *Has the financial crisis shattered citizens' trust in national and European governmental institutions? Evidence from the EU member states, 1999–2010*. CESP (Centre for European Policy Studies). https://EconPapers.repec.org/RePEc:eps:cepswp:4159

Roudometof, V. (2016). Theorizing glocalization: Three interpretations. *European Journal of Social Theory*, *19*(3), 391–408.
Sá, M. J., & Serpa, S. (2020). The COVID-19 pandemic as an opportunity to foster the sustainable development of teaching in higher education. *Sustainability*, *12*(20), 8525. https://doi.org/10.3390/su12208525
Shaluf, I. M., Ahmadun, F., & Mat Said, A. (2003), A review of disaster and crisis. *Disaster Prevention and Management*, *12*(1), 24–32. https://doi.org/10.1108/09653560310463829
Shen, S. Y., & Shaw, M. J. (2004, August 6–8) *Managing coordination in emergency response systems with information technologies*. In *10th Americas conference on information systems*, New York.
Stockemer, D., Niemann, A., Unger, D., & Speyer, J. (2020). The 'refugee crisis,' immigration attitudes, and euroscepticism. *International Migration Review*, *54*(3), 883–912. https://doi.org/10.1177/0197918319879926
Taggart, P., & Pirro, A. L. (2021). European populism before the pandemic: Ideology, Euroscepticism, electoral performance, and government participation of 63 parties in 30 countries. *Italian Political Science Review/Rivista Italiana Di Scienza Politica*, *51*(3), 281–304. https://doi.org/10.1017/ipo.2021.13
Usherwood, S. (2018). The third era of British Euroscepticism: Brexit as a paradigm shift. *The Political Quarterly*, *89*(4), 553–559. https://doi.org/10.1111/1467-923X.12598
Usherwood, S., & Startin, N. (2013). Euroscepticism as a persistent phenomenon. *JCMS: Journal of Common Market Studies*, *51*(1), 1–16. https://doi.org/10.1111/j.1468-5965.2012.02297.x
Wolbers, J., Kuipers, S., & Boin, A. (2021). A systematic review of 20 years of crisis and disaster research: Trends and progress. *Risk, Hazards & Crisis in Public Policy*, *12*(4), 374–392.
You, J. (2020). Lessons from South Korea's Covid-19 policy response. *The American Review of Public Administration*, *50*(6–7), 801–808. https://doi.org/10.1177/0275074020943708

Part II

Chapter 3

Assessing the Social Impact of an American Liberal Arts University: Implications and Challenges in the Post-conflict Society of Iraqi Kurdistan

Hayfa Jafar[a] and Munirah Eskander[b]

[a]Institutional Research & Strategic Insight Georgian College, Canada
[b]Sheikh Saud bin Saqr Al Qasimi Foundation for Policy Research, UAE

Abstract

In modern times, various American-style liberal arts universities have been established in conflict-affected states, including Iraqi Kurdistan. In the aftermath of the United States-led invasion of 2003, the majority of Iraq's universities were destroyed, which later provided further opportunities for the establishment of new higher education institutions, including those with an American-style university model. Taking the American University of Iraq, Sulaimani (AUIS) as a case study, this chapter explores the social impact of universities in post-conflict settings, including the impact of the cultural, communal, and research centres affiliated with the university. Using Onyx's (2014) conceptual framework of impact as an interpretive lens, interviews were conducted with nine professionals working at AUIS, five affiliated centres, and at an academic preparatory programme (APP). The findings demonstrate that participants perceive their initiatives and programmes to have a generally positive social impact such as by promoting policy dialogue, instigating social change, promoting community services, preserving cultural traditions, and building capacity. Nonetheless,

---

Education and Sustainable Development in the Context of Crises:
International Case Studies of Transformational Change, 25–43
Copyright © 2025 by Hayfa Jafar and Munirah Eskander. Published by Emerald Publishing Limited. These works are published under the Creative Commons Attribution (CC BY 4.0) licence. Anyone may reproduce, distribute, translate and create derivative works of these works (for both commercial and non-commercial purposes), subject to full attribution to the original publication and authors. The full terms of this licence may be seen at http://creativecommons.org/licenses/by/4.0/legalcode
doi:10.1108/978-1-83797-773-420241003

some issues limit the social impact of the initiatives undertaken, including communication challenges, limited funding, an unclear institutional vision, individualised efforts for community improvement, and the Kurdish community's hesitancy to accept AUIS' values and more liberal endeavours. Accordingly, we argue that the lack of clarity pertaining to AUIS' institutional identity and limited collaboration or communication between the university and its organisational affiliates, among other challenges, have limited the social impact of the university and its outreach within the Kurdish community in Iraq.

Keywords: Post-conflict society; social impact; critical thinking; American-style university; liberal arts

3.1 Introduction

In modern times, many American-style liberal arts universities have been established in countries that have undergone a regime change or experienced conflict (Godwin, 2015; Jafar, 2023; Long, 2020). Such universities have adopted a system associated with political and social liberalisation as well as the enhancement of citizenry's agency, especially in the post-communist era (van der Wende, 2011). Additionally, these institutions help to equip youth with critical thinking skills (Becker, 2015) while providing the expertise needed to rebuild a country (Long, 2018). In effect, introducing a liberal arts curriculum to supplement professional and technical programmes can help with 're-establishing the balance between breadth and depth of knowledge' (van der Wende, 2011, p. 24), especially in a post-conflict society such as Iraq.

Over the past few decades, Iraq has been devastated by various political and sectarian conflicts since the overthrow of Saddam Hussain and his authoritarian Ba'ath party following the invasion led by the United States in 2003. By 2005, estimates suggested that roughly 84% of Iraqi universities were destroyed and looted, particularly in central Iraq (United Nations University, 2005). However, further damage was inflicted upon higher education institutions by various non-state actors, including the Islamic State of Iraq and Syria (ISIS), between 2014 and 2019. Accordingly, however, such events, especially the 2003 invasion, created opportunities to establish American-style universities that are supported politically and financially by the United States as part of a broader project to 'promote' democratic and liberal values in post-conflict states (Milton, 2013). The American-style university model intends to help unite ethnic and religious groups by employing a liberal arts curriculum to nurture inclusive leadership that acknowledges and promotes the diversity of Iraqi society within what is purportedly a pluralistic democracy. This is achieved mainly by exposing students to Western democratic values, emphasising the rights of minorities, and ensuring they receive a well-rounded education (Long, 2018).

In modern history, higher education systems have evolved to promote knowledge production and transmission while further catalysing socio-political, economic, and cultural change. Many studies have suggested that universities may be able to positively impact national processes of reconciliation, identity building, and socio-political change, which are critical for the recovery of post-conflict societies (e.g., Agasisti, 2009; Hopkins, 2011; Temple, 2008). As war and organised violence continue to afflict countries around the world, perceptions of higher education have changed in conflict and post-conflict settings (Milton & Barakat, 2016; Pacheco, 2013). In cases where conflict has ended, higher education has been seen as a catalyst for recovery, stabilisation and securitisation, state building, and peacebuilding (Milton & Barakat, 2016). However, universities are normally influenced by external and internal forces that could reduce their impact on society. Nevertheless, some conditions could shift the dynamics of these forces and help initiate change in established practices (Burch, 2007).

Since universities mirror and often drive many political, military, economic, and social changes (Feuer et al., 2013), it is important to study the intangible social impact of higher education within the context of conflict. Hence, this chapter aims to explore the intended (or unintended) social impact of universities in post-conflict contexts, such as Iraqi Kurdistan, taking the AUIS as a case study. Unintended impacts are effects that are not specified in the statement of institutional objectives or result from activities beyond a planned programme or initiative (Onyx, 2014). Some common unintended impacts or risks of higher education in a post-conflict society are brain drain, political instability where universities often become a space for politically active students and academics to initiate protest and political movements, and the risk of political violence (Milton & Barakat, 2016).

Moreover, Feuer et al. (2013) suggest that, as sites of knowledge production and contestation, universities can become a battleground for the emergence of new political entities. They argue that the process of reconstructing higher education also carries the risk of perpetuating ethnic and class tensions, potentially leading to a resurgence of violence or conflict. In addition, curricula and teaching materials may not always be tailored to the specific needs and challenges of the post-conflict society, leading to a mismatch between the education provided and the society's needs (Milton, 2018). Accordingly, while universities may potentially unite and reform societies, it is unclear whether an American-style university model adopted in a foreign, post-conflict context such as Iraqi Kurdistan can fulfil its hypothesised outcome and purpose. Thus, this chapter aims to explore the social impact of an American-style university in a post-conflict setting, taking AUIS as a case study, including the impact of the cultural, communal, and research centres affiliated with the university.

Additionally, this chapter delves into an examination of how broader cultural and political influences approach certain practices associated with the core values of the university, such as the promotion of critical thinking and gender equality. Therefore, the central research question addressed in this chapter is: *To what extent do the research, communal, and cultural centres affiliated with the AUIS have an impact on Kurdish society?*

The structure of this chapter is as follows: In the following section, we will provide an overview of the case study followed by a literature review that outlines the role of higher education in post-conflict settings, while further reflecting on the topic of American-style universities. Next, we outline the conceptual framework used to guide our research, adopting Onyx's (2014) framework and dimensions pertaining to 'impact'. The section that follows describes the methodology, focusing, in particular, on interviews conducted with individuals working in AUIS as well as its organisational affiliates. Then, we provide an overview of the research and communal centres affiliated with the university. This is followed by a discussion of the themes that emerged from the data analysis, spotlighting challenges faced by these entities in attempting to leave an impact on society. Lastly, the conclusion summarises the contributions of this chapter.

3.2 An Overview: AUIS

AUIS is located in a region known as the birthplace of ancient civilisations, characterised by sectarian political structures, diverse peoples, and a history of conflict. It was founded by the Kurdish-Iraqi politician Barham Salih, the appointed president of Iraq between 2018 and 2022, former prime minister of the Kurdistan region between 2009 and 2012, and former deputy prime minister of the Iraqi federal government from 2006 to 2009. AUIS offers various undergraduate programmes in engineering, technology, business, and the social sciences, supplemented by a liberal arts curriculum (core programme). It further promotes inter- and multidisciplinary education and focuses on student learning objectives related to written and oral communication, numeracy, and critical thinking skills (AUIS, n.d.-a). The mission of AUIS is to instil a sense of communal responsibility in its graduates, further equipping them with the knowledge and core skills needed to become competent professionals and leaders. Its core values include freedom and responsibility, democracy, freedom of expression and inquiry, equal opportunity, individual rights, tolerance, and honourable personal and professional behaviour (AUIS, n.d.-a).

According to Salih, AUIS was established in post-conflict Iraq, specifically in the Kurdistan region, to support peace efforts, national unity, democracy, leadership, and post-conflict reform (Moulakis, 2011; Wong 2007). Salih argued that education is key to the future of the region and identified the liberal arts component of the university as necessary to cultivate tolerance, solidarity, and progressive thinking among students (AUIS Official, 2016). The justifications for fostering peace and social cohesion also explain the inclusion of 'Iraq' in the university's name, which legitimises continued financial and political support locally, regionally, and internationally. Furthermore, it aligns with the 2003 American invasion agenda of 'liberating' Iraq as a country (Long, 2018).

The political rationale for establishing American-style universities, in particular, such as AUIS, is often described as a soft power tactic to disseminate American values. It has further been utilised by the US government to promote American public diplomacy objectives in various ways (e.g., to counter anti-American sentiment) (Bertelsen, 2012, 2014; Moulakis, 2011). As a relatively young university, inaugurated in 2007 amid significant political shifts in Iraq, it continues to struggle with establishing a firm foundation in a region grappling with ongoing conflicts. Moreover, political and economic instability has been exacerbated by the devastation caused by ISIS since 2014 and the outbreak of COVID-19 in 2019.

Aside from offering APPs and undergraduate- and graduate-level degrees, AUIS strives to make meaningful contributions to society. For example, various research, communal, and cultural centres have been established for this purpose, including the Institute of Regional and International Studies (IRIS) and the Center for Gender and Development Studies (CGDS). As such, this chapter endeavours to explore and present empirical evidence regarding the social impact of AUIS, especially its organisational affiliates. It pays particular attention to the latter's attempts to maximise their impact on Kurdish society, as well as how they are influenced by and adapt to the changing dynamics of their environment. This chapter also explores any potential disparities between the university's stated objectives and its actual practices that diminish its impact on Kurdish society.

3.3 Literature Review: The Social Role of Universities

Over the past decade, an expanding body of research has emerged on the positive role of higher education in conflict-affected, fragile, and post-war contexts. Existing research has primarily focused on how to rebuild, reform, or protect the sector and on how higher education can contribute to post-conflict recovery (Milton & Barakat, 2016; Pacheco, 2013). However, it is undeniable that measuring or quantifying the social impact of higher education is challenging, largely because it is difficult to define, time-consuming, and tends to be more qualitative than quantitative. In addition, it is complex and likely holds varying meanings in different contexts (Onyx, 2014).

Nevertheless, it is crucial to engage in the debate about the role of universities in societies, particularly in fragile societies impacted by conflicts. For instance, Milton and Barakat (2016) examine the relationship between higher education and four core intervention agendas in conflict-affected societies: stabilisation and securitisation, reconstruction, state building, and peacebuilding. Many other authors stress the importance of universities in promoting intercultural dialogue (Nahas, 2008) and social critique (Qureshi, 2008) as part of the peacebuilding process. Moreover, universities are seen as a space for expressing new ideas and infusing cultural openness in otherwise closed societies, while also viewed as a tool for the preservation of local or national cultures (Brennan et al., 2004). Furthermore, other studies found that exposing students to different ideas can break down negative stereotypes based on, for example, differences in ethnicity, race, religion, gender, or socioeconomic status (Sagy, 2002; Tomovska, 2010). Moreover, through various initiatives by governments, nongovernmental organisations (NGOs), students, and faculty, universities have been instrumental in providing access to education to various traditionally marginalised social groups, such as peasants and labourers (Pacheco, 2013). More recently, following the ongoing Russian invasion of Ukraine in February 2022,

Kushnir (2023) concluded that higher education is increasingly serving as a foundation for political collaboration, extending beyond its education role to foster peace in the European region.

Brannelly et al. (2011) further view campuses as arenas of political socialisation, where individuals gain knowledge about how political and social systems operate. In addition, they develop an understanding of their political culture, system of shared values, and ideologies about institutions within their societies. However, other studies have found that this ideal impact of universities is not always achieved due to various institutional, political, and economic factors. For instance, Tahirsylaj (2008) argues that the higher education system in Kosovo remains divided along ethnic lines, and the main challenge in developing modern, open-minded, cohesive institutions is that some universities try to promote 'nationalistic agendas', thereby limiting opportunities for peacebuilding and reconciliation.

Similarly, Feuer et al. (2013) argue that the potential for campuses to achieve peacebuilding outcomes, such as long-term integration, intercultural communication, and tolerance building, largely depends on the university and its administrators' ability to create a welcoming campus environment. The authors examined university spaces, such as campuses and student cultural institutions, as well as the projections of university administrators on social hierarchy in five post-conflict societies. They found that administrators' limited capacity or willingness for change, due to various political reasons, served as barriers to achieving the expected impact.

Beyond higher education in post-conflict settings, more generally, the literature on American-style universities, more specifically, examines a wide range of themes. A few studies have explored the opportunities, challenges, and impacts this university model brings to its host country. For example, Ghabra and Arnold (2007) stated that the main effect that American-style universities have had is in forming a class of elites in countries and regions in which they were established. This university model has also proved pivotal in introducing and strengthening critical thinking skills, serving as a centre for civil society in an otherwise authoritarian political landscape (Noori & Anderson, 2013). Purinton and Skaggs (2017) further argue that American-style universities have been modernising their host countries for decades. Similarly, Jafar and Sabzalieva (2022) found that establishing American-style universities is seen by different stakeholders as a fast track towards building the academic reputations of national higher education systems, particularly in post-conflict societies.

This brief literature review demonstrates the scholarly consensus that higher education institutions play a vital role in promoting peace, reconciliation, development, political socialisation, and social integration in post-conflict societies. Nevertheless, there is a dearth of empirical evidence regarding their impact in such societies, as well as the internal and external challenges and barriers that impede the maximisation of this theorised impact. Therefore, this chapter offers an alternative perspective on the social impact of universities in post-conflict contexts, which is discussed further below, by focusing primarily on the American liberal arts university model.

3.4 Conceptual Framework

Defining and measuring the intangible societal-level impact of universities is a complex endeavour. Each university defines its social impact differently based on its mission and core values. For example, Universities Canada defines social impact as 'the positive outcomes of initiatives that tackle social, economic, environmental, and cultural challenges faced by people, organisations, and communities' (Universities Canada, n.d.). The University of Michigan further defines social impact as 'a significant, positive change that addresses a pressing social challenge' (University of Michigan, n.d.). Generally, different terms are used to refer to impact such as 'returns', 'benefits', and 'value' (Penfield et al., 2014), which assume that a positive or beneficial effect will be considered as an impact. Nevertheless, this impact, as discussed above, encompasses multiple dimensions and can be either positive or negative as well as intended or unintended (Arvidson, 2009; Onyx, 2014), especially within post-conflict societies.

For the purpose of this study, we utilise Onyx's (2014) conceptual framework of impact as a lens to interpret the social impact of AUIS. Whereas Onyx's model of social impact is applicable to social organisations, we adapt her model and apply it to the higher education institution of AUIS and its affiliates. Our interpretation of her framework further involves narrowing down her seven propositions to four key dimensions. The first dimension pertains to the university's core values and networks embedded in its liberal arts model, especially the notions of critical thinking, leadership, diversity, and enhancing citizens' agency. The second dimension emphasises how broader contribution to a local community occurs as a result of university practices and active communal networks. We investigate this feature by examining the contributions of the centres affiliated with AUIS.

Individual engagement and development constitute the third dimension, which underscores the institutional culture and individuals' agency in promoting or bringing about societal changes and developing their capacity to do so. The final dimension is 'dual-level impact', which examines the extent to which the university and its students, faculty, management, and staff are embedded within the local community and how the community supports and strengthens the university. It pertains to the idea that the university and its individual stakeholders are an integral part of the larger social structure, thereby being influenced by the norms, values, and dynamics of the society they belong to.

As discussed by Onyx (2014), this conceptual framework does not in itself provide a measure of social impact; however, it offers a lens to interpret and analyse institutional activities to measure their social impact quantitatively and qualitatively. Moreover, it identifies the gap between the university's intended impact, as communicated in the mission statements of the research, cultural, and communal centres, and their concrete output. It also allows for problematising and exploring the intended and unintended, positive and negative impacts of the university's initiatives and programmes. While Onyx's conceptualisation of impact does not specifically pertain to higher education institutions and instead focuses on various communal and civil society organisations more broadly, we have adapted her

Table 3.1. Interviewee Themes and Onyx's Dimensions.

No.	Onyx's Dimension	Themes
1	Core values and networks	Communication challenges; unclear institutional vision
2	Contributions to the local community	Unclear institutional vision; lack of funding; communication challenges
3	Individual engagement and development	Individual efforts; lack of funding
4	Dual-level impact	Communication challenges; unclear institutional vision; lack of funding; individual efforts; Kurdish community's hesitancy

understanding to that of universities and its organisational affiliates. Accordingly, we then utilised Onyx's dimensions to identify the themes that emerged from the interview data (see Table 3.1).

3.5 Methodology

This research relies on the qualitative analysis of a case study to investigate the societal impact of the American-style university model implemented in the post-2003 Iraqi-Kurdish context. The research design and data collection of this study was informed by the Institutional Review Board Guidebook and followed a favourable ethics decision from the AUIS. It approved the non-anonymising of the name of the university that we used as a case study.

The chosen case study of AUIS exemplifies an American-style institution established in a post-conflict society. While AUIS operates as an independent, not-for-profit entity, it holds the legal status of a private university and falls under the regulatory control of both the Ministry of Higher Education and Scientific Research in Kurdistan and central Iraq (AUIS, n.d.).

Semi-structured interviews were conducted as part of this case study. Interview questions were designed based on the social impact framework developed by Onyx (2014), aiming to capture participants' experiences within American-style universities, with a specific emphasis on (1) core values and networks, (2) contributions to the local community, (3) individual engagement and development, and (4) dual-level impact. The study involved interviews with nine participants, comprising employees and researchers working at the university; five research, communal, and cultural centres; and at the APP affiliated with AUIS (see Table 3.2). Most of the participants actively lead various community service initiatives and programmes.

In addition to the interviews, information from the university website and the web pages of the organisational affiliates have been used to complement the analysis.

The process of thematic data analysis commenced with coding and identifying categories, which were determined based on the participants' perspectives regarding the social impact of their respective centres and programmes. This involved examining recurring patterns in the data across participants, ultimately leading to the emergence of categories and their interrelationships, offering explanations for the participants' views on the social impact of the American-style university model in a post-conflict society.

The Institutional Review Board at the university granted permission to conduct the study.

The study has a few limitations, in that only a few individuals from AUIS, its organisational affiliates, and APP were interviewed. In addition, due to the limited availability of data, other quantitative analysis was not conducted to measure the impact of the programmes and initiatives carried out on the ground since 2007. Accordingly, additional semi-structured interviews, analysis of the scope and reach of initiatives, and measurement of the receptiveness of the Kurdish public to these programmes could provide greater insight into the impact of AUIS and its affiliates in future studies. The following section provides an overview of the scope of work of AUIS' different organisational affiliates and APP programme, while further discussing the interview data below.

3.6 Organisational Affiliates of AUIS

As noted above in Table 3.2, one of the key research institutes affiliated with AUIS is IRIS, a policy dialogue centre that focuses on conducting research on issues relevant to Iraq and the wider Middle East and North African region. By further hosting events related to policy dialogue, IRIS researchers liaise with other academics to bring key issues related to climate change, the environment, and civilian protection, among others, to the forefront. The centre has further hosted workshops and seminars to aid in the capacity building of youth in AUIS, including hosting the first workshop for Iraq Leadership Fellows in 2023 (AUIS, n.d.-b).

Another centre that engages in research in relation to societal change is the CGDS, which prioritises holding up values pertaining to equality and fairness. Among its many accomplishments, the CGDS has set up the first gender studies minor in the country, while further funding research projects pertaining to gender and sexuality, including masculinity and how it influences social interactions between men and women. A segment of the CGDS further focuses on disability rights in Sulaymaniyah, leading to the establishment of the first disability studies minor in the country as well. The CGDS also offered funding to gender scholars, sponsoring 'Jan Warner Visiting Scholars' and facilitating their teaching of gender courses at the university (AUIS, n.d.-c).

Aside from societal and political change, AUIS has also promoted economic development through the AEIC, which is a centre founded in 2019 that prioritises the empowerment of entrepreneurs. In the attempt to tackle challenges affiliated with poor infrastructure and few mentorship opportunities in the city, among others, AEIC offers entrepreneurs various forms of support, including mentors,

Table 3.2. Overview of AUIS Organisational Affiliates and Programmes.

No.	AUIS Organisational Affiliates and Programmes	Objective
1	IRIS	Serves as a policy research and training centre.
2	CGDS	Helps empower men and women through education and research.
3	The AUIS Entrepreneurship and Innovation Centre (AEIC)	Supports Iraqi/Kurdish entrepreneurs by creating a helpful, scalable ecosystem through research, education, networking, and partnerships.
4	AUIS Center for Archaeology and Cultural Heritage (CACHE)	Preserves and raises awareness of Iraqi/Kurdish cultural heritage and archaeological sites.
5	Kashkul – Centre for Arts and Culture	Aims to protect artistic and cultural expression and material.
6	APP – Community Outreach	Aids community outreach through supporting teacher professional development, training high school students, and developing English proficiency of marginalised individuals.

funding, and resources to aid their growth and development. Moreover, it has launched a business accelerator called Takween, which has the capacity to aid dozens of entrepreneurial ventures across the country (AUIS, n.d.-d).

In accordance with Iraq's rich cultural heritage, the university has further established CACHE to promote the protection and development of cultural and historical sites across Kurdistan and Iraq more broadly. By offering training sessions to youth and adopting a scientific approach to Iraqi history, various technologies are adopted by this centre to protect cultural heritage sites from looting and/or other violent non-state actors that seek to profit from or destroy buildings or historical areas (AUIS, n.d.-e).

The last centre founded to support artistic and cultural expression is Kaskhul, which attempts to preserve cultural and historical artistic works in Iraqi Kurdistan. Established in 2016, Kaskhul's projects have ranged from the artistic or cultural to the literary, and the centre works on hosting arts events, curating arts exhibitions, and hosting other events at the university. As one of the longest standing centres affiliated with AUIS, Kaskhul has supported the publishing of over 2,000 pages of translated literature in the attempt to make it more accessible to the international community. It further supports artistic and cultural events, including the first-ever Sulaimani Festival for Culture and Art, held in September 2023 (Kashkul, n.d.).

Lastly, while not a centre, APP serves as an important programme that supports the professional development of high school teachers in Sulaymaniyah, where instructors prioritise student-centred pedagogies in their overall approach to teaching. By working closely together with non-native English-speaking students, the APP programme instructors endeavour to teach the former 'academic English, critical thinking skills and study habits' (AUIS, n.d.-f).

In sum, this programme and all of AUIS' organisational affiliates seek to have an impact on society by promoting policy dialogue about pressing issues in Iraq, supporting local entrepreneurs, preserving local culture, bringing awareness about social issues, and building the capacity of both enrolled students and teachers as well as other community members in general.

3.7 Findings and Discussion

This section provides an overview and analyses the key themes that emerged during our interviews with both university staff and employees working at AUIS' organisational affiliates. As noted earlier, a total of nine professionals at AUIS, its organisational affiliates, and APP were interviewed to better evaluate the extent to which these centres have impacted Kurdish society. Our interviews revealed that various obstacles hinder the social impact of these centres, largely due to five observations pertaining to (1) communication challenges, (2) an unclear institutional vision and inconsistent strategies, (3) limited funding, (4) individual efforts for community betterment, and (5) the Kurdish community's hesitancy to accept AUIS' values and more liberal initiatives.

3.7.1 Communication Challenges

One of the most common themes that emerged in the majority of interviews pertained to communication challenges taking place at the internal level. According to one interviewee from AEIC,

> [...] Given the small size of AUIS, to me, it's unacceptable that AUIS lacks internal communications and synergy.

Since most centres function independently of the university, the AUIS management is not involved in how the centres conduct research, disseminate knowledge, acquire funding from donors, or offer training outside of or on campus. In addition, workshop organisers from organisational affiliates do not receive feedback from the university, such as in relation to who to invite for guest lectures. While the management does not interfere with or discourage planned activities, they do not provide input or facilitate any such initiatives.

The instances in which communication between the centres and AUIS takes place are largely when events are being planned due to the need to obtain security clearance, such as to host a workshop. In addition, the centres must also communicate with the university to pay money to host events on campus. However, no monitoring and evaluation efforts have been put into place by the university to measure the impact of the activities or initiatives offered by the centres. Accordingly, employees spoken to from each of the respective centres indicated that beyond providing security clearance and paying to rent a space at AUIS for events, communication between the university and the organisational affiliates is relatively limited and focused on offering logistical support. Thus, to maximise the social impact of AUIS and its organisational affiliates, greater internal communication must take place to enable collaborative endeavours that can better support the community.

3.7.2 Unclear Institutional Vision and Inconsistent Strategies

A second emerging theme from the majority of interviews pertained to different perceptions of the university's vision or purpose among its employees. While the university promotes certain liberal core values, which have been discussed earlier in this chapter, many of the individuals in the university do not ascribe to these values. According to an interviewee from the AEIC,

> AUIS lacks a clear strategy, clear set of principles, and a clear vision of what kind of institution of education it wants to become.

This is further confirmed by an interviewee from the CGDS, who stated that many core staff and faculty members disagree with and criticise the university's liberal core values which can affect the role it plays as an agent of change, creating a tense atmosphere within AUIS. For example, some staff oppose the work of the CGDS due to their more conservative beliefs. Thus, according to this interviewee, gender equality is not promoted in a harmonious manner within the classroom, and there is no consistent messaging pertaining to advocacy and the pursuit of social change. This further applies to marginalised communities or individuals. According to one employee, the university does not sufficiently accommodate persons with disabilities through the creation of physically accessible infrastructure or provision of educational resources.

However, another interviewed staff member from the university indicated that

> [...] Social development, per se is not typically the goal of a university or any educational establishment. Instead, we are trying to educate.

The interviewee additionally clarified later on that the university is

> [...] extremely careful not to define AUIS as a social agent. We are not here to change people's ideas about religion, or about how they want to do their government, or how they, in fact, farm their fields.

Instead, the interviewee argued that the social impact of AUIS must be identified by its alumni and the change they create in society. The individual posits that while they (the alumni) are the ones who will adapt and implement what they have learned, the university cannot measure this impact easily. Hence, there is no sustainability or consistency regarding the internal processes of data collection to measure impact or connect with alumni to receive any feedback from them. The most reliable way to address this issue is by obtaining anecdotal evidence from alumni and AUIS employers.

Accordingly, these perspectives illustrate that AUIS staff and organisational affiliates perceive of social change and *who* is responsible for instigating this differently, demonstrating an inconsistent vision between the centres and university staff. Hence, in order to strengthen the impact of the university, it must adopt a more uniform institutional identity and be more consistent in communicating its strategies and representing its vision internally across its centres and programmes.

3.7.3 Limited Funding

The third recurring theme that was noted by all centres as well as university staff pertained to challenges related to attaining sufficient funding to conduct research and run their programmatic activities or other initiatives. This is specifically connected to the absence of sufficient funding at the local level. In the words of one university staff member,

> There's no funding for research in Iraq, so that stops the pipeline…The only way we managed to do that [research] is getting funding from outside Iraq, and that often comes with strings, you know, it's project oriented.

Accordingly, for example, the AEIC's Takween Accelerator receives funding from the European Union and the Ministry of Foreign Affairs in France (AUIS, 2020). In addition, the CGDS also obtained funding from the London School of Economics, based in the United Kingdom, to investigate the construction of masculinity in Kurdish society (AUIS, 2019).

Limited funding also affects dissemination efforts, where much of the work carried out by these affiliated centres – such as publications, workshops, and events – is in English. As such, the programmes, resources, and other initiatives are not accessible to the wider Kurdish/Arab community without translators, which also requires funding. Hence, the challenges associated with the acquisition of external funding are exacerbated by the need to disseminate knowledge in the local language and pay the university to rent a space for events. According to all interviewees, AUIS treats its centres as financial resources, not as initiatives for social engagement or social impact. Thus, the work conducted by these organisations can and *does* have an impact; however, this is limited due to financial considerations pertaining to dissemination (among other) expenses. While the university and its organisational affiliates clearly have an impact on society, it would be helpful if the relationship between AUIS and its centres, in particular, was to become more collaborative and supportive instead of transactional to better maximise their social impact.

3.7.4 Individual and Personal Efforts for Community Betterment

The fourth theme that emerged from the majority of interviews pertains to the emphasis on the individual and personal efforts of the employees themselves. For example, they indicated that they often rely on their personal connections and networks to apply for grants, set up events, disseminate knowledge, and engage with the local community. Both faculty and employees at centres explained that much of the work that they do requires them to be proactive and can also involve expenditure that is not covered by the university. For example, one interviewee mentioned that experiential learning field trips are not facilitated by the university and the faculty themselves must organise and pay for the transportation for students. In addition, the number of communal outreach activities carried out in recent years has decreased significantly, with one employee from CACHE stating,

> We used to work much more closely with NGOs, we used to work on refugee projects and work in the refugee camps, there was a real excitement to be out there doing projects, with people who actually need support.

The individual further emphasised,

> We have to expand the number of such issues by engaging students on and get[ting] them out of the classroom into the community, meeting these people.

This demonstrates that the shift away from richer, more student-centred pedagogical approaches through experiential learning depends largely on the individual efforts of instructors. Accordingly, the university's provision of greater support to faculty and employees of affiliated centres and APP could enrich the experiences of students while also easing the pressure placed on employees and staff. In turn, this could further maximise the impact that such activities have on the wider community, such as the field trips undertaken to support refugees mentioned above.

3.7.5 Kurdish Community's Hesitancy to Accept Liberal Values

The fifth theme pertains to the Kurdish community's hesitancy to embrace AUIS' liberal values and initiatives. Despite the university's prestigious standing and reputation as a legitimate institution of higher education and its recognition for its impactful work, it is still criticised for having a perceived Western agenda that serves its external donors to the detriment of Kurdish values and traditions. This is particularly applicable to CGDS, which was viewed as a threat to traditional understandings of gender relations in Iraqi Kurdistan. According to an interviewee from CGDS, the community is also suspicious of the sources of external funding as well as how money acquired from donors is spent, with the interviewee stating that there are conspiracy theories suggesting that they are being funded as NGOs and academic centres to 'destroy' the Kurdish community.

However, it is important to note that an AUIS staff member indicated that the university supports its faculty, stating

> When our faculty or staff are doing the right thing ... if they get attacked, from the outside, this university will line up behind them. And it may not be public, it may not be highly visible, but we line up behind them.

Nonetheless, other interviewees from centres aside from CGDS noted that they remain wary of engaging in more controversial community outreach. According to an interviewee from AEIC,

> Interestingly, AUIS seems to be known across the country for being an American liberal university, sometimes for good sometimes for bad. Probably, you are aware of the, let's say, disputes or resentments that came up against some of the activities and programmes from the Gender Centre. And sometimes internally, we are not aware of what the other centres do, but it seems like somebody in Baghdad and somebody in Amarah and somebody in Basra is actually following AUIS and is making a video on it as well.

Accordingly, to build trust between the community and AUIS and its organisational affiliates, the university must devise strategies to decrease the community's suspicion of the activities undertaken by its affiliates. Moreover, it must take more steps to correct misconceptions that the general public may have about these initiatives and the sources of funding in order to better support community members and meet their needs.

3.8 Conclusion

The establishment of American-style liberal arts universities has taken place in numerous countries around the world, including within the post-conflict society of Iraqi Kurdistan. In this case, the founding of AUIS and its organisational affiliates has not come without challenges. For this study, we have utilised Onyx's (2014) conceptual framework of impact as a lens to inform our investigation of the extent to which AUIS; its research, communal, and cultural centres; and APP have had an impact on Kurdish society.

Based on the interviews, AUIS and its organisational affiliates have had a positive impact on Kurdish society through the various initiatives they have undertaken to support community outreach efforts. However, five challenges pertaining to communication, institutional vision, funding, individualisation of efforts, and resistance from the Kurdish community have reduced the impact of the university and its organisational affiliates. These challenges have negatively affected the university's ability to adhere to its institutional identity and core values as a liberal arts institution, while further limiting its contributions to the local community. Hence, while the individual efforts of employees working in AUIS' organisational affiliates have not necessarily met with resistance, they have received limited support from the university's administration. Coupled with the Kurdish society's hesitancy to accept or embrace the values and standing of the university on multiple issues, this matter has limited the impact of the university and its affiliated centres and programmes.

Accordingly, we argue that the limited social impact of these centres has led them to be placed in a precarious position caught in the middle between Kurdish society and AUIS. Due to the suspicions of the community of some of AUIS' values and initiatives, exacerbated by somewhat limited support from the university's staff, AUIS may be drifting away from what made it uniquely placed to address key social issues in Iraqi Kurdistan, namely, its liberal arts identity.

Declaration of Conflicting Interests

The authors declare no potential conflicts of interest with respect to the research, authorship, and/or publication of this study.

Funding

The authors received no financial support for the research, authorship, and/or publication of this study.

Ethical Approval

The research design and data collection of this study was informed by the Institutional Review Board Guidebook and followed a favourable ethics decision from the American University of Iraq, Sulaimani.

Informed Consent

Written informed consent was obtained from all participants prior to the interviews.

References

Agasisti, T. (2009). Towards 'Lisbon objectives': Economic determinants of participation rates in university education: An empirical analysis in 14 European countries. *Higher Education Quarterly*, *63*(3), 287–307. https://doi.org/10.1111/j.1468-2273.2008.00416.x

Arvidson, M. (2009). *Impact and evaluation in the UK third sector: Reviewing literature and exploring ideas*. Working Paper No. 27. https://eprints.soton.ac.uk/183217/1/arvidson_working_paper_27.pdf

AUIS. (2019, June 19). London School of Economics selects AUIS as a lead institutional research partner. AUIS. Retrieved November 17, 2023, from https://auis.edu.krd/?q=news/london-school-economics-selectsauislead-institutional-research-partner

AUIS. (2020, July 9). *AUIS entrepreneurship initiative and Yanhad project launch Iraq's first business accelerator*. AUIS. Retrieved November 17, 2023, from https://auis.edu.krd/?q=news/auis-entrepreneurshipinitiative-and-yanhad-project-launch-iraq%E2%80%99s-first-business-accelerator

AUIS. (n.d.-a). Mission and values. Retrieved November 17, 2023, from https://auis.edu.krd/?q=mission-and-values

AUIS. (n.d.-b). *AUIS Institute of Regional and International Studies*. Retrieved November 17, 2023, from https://auis.edu.krd/iris/

AUIS. (n.d.-c). *The Center for Gender and Development Studies*. Retrieved November 17, 2023, from https://auis.edu.krd/CGDS/

AUIS. (n.d.-d). *Entrepreneurship and Innovation Center*. Retrieved November 17, 2023, from https://auis.edu.krd/aeic/

AUIS. (n.d.-e). Center for Archaeology and Cultural Heritage. Retrieved November 17, 2023, from https://auis.edu.krd/cache/

AUIS. (n.d.-f). *Academic preparatory program*. Retrieved November 17, 2023, from https://www.auis.edu.krd/app-home/

AUIS Official. (2016, April 3). *AUIS founding: Reforming higher education* [Video file]. YouTube. Retrieved November 17, 2023, from https://www.youtube.com/watch?v=am7yIwRftyE

Becker, J. (2015). Liberal arts and sciences education: Responding to the challenges of the XXIst century. *Voprosy Obrazovaniya/Educational Studies, 4*, 33–61. https://doi.org/10.17323/1814-9545-2015-4-33-61

Bertelsen, R. G. (2012). Private foreign-affiliated universities, the state, and soft power: The American University of Beirut and the American University in Cairo. *Foreign Policy Analysis, 8*(3), 293–311. https://doi.org/10.1111/j.1743-8594.2011.00163.x

Bertelsen, R. G. (2014). The university as a transnational actor with transnational power: American missionary universities in the Middle East and China. *PS: Political Science & Politics, 47*(3), 624–627. https://doi.org/10.1017/S1049096514000754

Brannelly, L., Lewis, L., & Ndaruhutse, S. (2011). Higher education and the formation of developmental elites. Developmental Leadership Program (DLP). http://www.dlprog.org/ftp/view/Public%20Folder/1%20Research%20Papers/Higher%20education%20and%20the%20formation%20of%20developmental%20elites.pdf

Brennan, J., King, R., & Lebeau, Y. (2004). *The role of universities in the transformation of societies: An international research project: Synthesis report*. Association of Commonwealth Universities and Centre for Higher Education Research and Information. ISBN 0 7492 0513 X.

Burch, P. (2007). Educational policy and practice from the perspective of institutional theory: Crafting a wider lens. *Educational Researcher, 36*(2), 84–95. https://doi.org/10.3102/0013189X07299792

Feuer, H. N., Hornidge, A. K., & Schetter, C. (2013). *Rebuilding knowledge: Opportunities and risks for higher education in post-conflict regions*. ZEF Working Paper No. 121. https://www.econstor.eu/bitstream/10419/88345/1/773540326.pdf

Ghabra, S., & Arnold, M. (2007, June). Studying the American way: An assessment of American-style higher education in Arab countries. The Washington Institute for Near East Policy. https://www.washingtoninstitute.org/policy-analysis/view/studying-the-americanway-an-assessment-of-american-style-higher-education.

Godwin, K. A. (2015). The worldwide emergence of liberal education. *International Higher Education, 79*, 2–4. https://doi.org/10.6017/ihe.2015.79.5835

Hopkins, P. (2011). Towards critical geographies of the university campus: Understanding the contested experiences of Muslim students. *Transactions of the Institute of British Geographers, 36*, 157–169. https://doi.org/10.1111/j.1475-5661.2010.00407.x

Jafar, H. (2023). Fertile ground for establishing American-style universities in post-conflict societies: Historical comparisons and current rationales. *Higher Education Policy*, 418–435. https://doi.org/10.1057/s41307-023-00312-5

Jafar, H., & Sabzalieva, E. (2022). Faculty experiences of higher education internationalization in post-conflict Iraq and Tajikistan. *Journal of Comparative and International Higher Education, 14*(2), 47–65.

Kashkul. (n.d.). Kashkul. Retrieved November 17, 2023, from https://www.kashkul.com/

Kushnir, I. (2023). 'It is more than just education. It's also a peace policy': (Re)imagining the mission of the European higher education area in the context of the Russian invasion of Ukraine. *European Educational Research Journal*. https://doi.org/10.1177/14749041231200927.

Long, K. A. (2018). *The emergence of the American university abroad*. Doctoral dissertation, Columbia University. Academic Commons.

Long, K. A. (2020). The emergence of the American university abroad. Brill Sense. ISBN 978 90-04-42576-7.

Milton, S. (2013). *The neglected pillar of recovery: A study of higher education in post-war Iraq and Libya*. Doctoral dissertation, University of York.

Milton, S. (2018). *Higher education and post-conflict recovery*. Palgrave Macmillan. ISBN 978-3-319-65349-5.

Milton, S., & Barakat, S. (2016). Higher education as a catalyst of recovery in conflict affected societies. *Globalization, Societies and Education, 14*(3), 403–421. ISBN 9780203710647.

Moulakis, A. (2011, July 3). What the U.S. government can't do abroad, colleges can. *Chronicle*. https://www.chronicle.com/article/what-the-u-s-government-cant-do-abroad colleges-ca/

Nahas, G. N. (2008). The university experience, a way to meet the other: A Lebanese case. In *Proceedings of the 4th international Barcelona conference on higher education*, Barcelona. http://web.guni2005.upc.es/media/0000000500/0000000539.pdf

Noori, N., & Anderson, P. K. (2013). Globalization, governance, and the diffusion of the American model of education: Accreditation agencies and American-style universities in the Middle East. *International Journal of Politics, Culture, and Society, 26*(2), 159–172. https://doi.org/10.1007/s10767-013-9131-1

Onyx, J. (2014). A theoretical model of social impact. *Cosmopolitan Civil Societies Journal, 6*(1), 1–18. https://search.informit.org/doi/10.3316/informit.929746443601599

Pacheco, I. (2013). *Conflict, post conflict, and functions of the university: Lessons from Colombia and other conflicts*. Doctoral dissertation, Boston College. eScholarship@ BC, Boston College University Libraries.

Penfield, T., Baker, M., Scoble, R., & Wykes, M. (2014). Assessment, evaluations, and definitions of research impact: A review. *Research Evaluation, 23*(1), 21–32, https://doi.org/10.1093/reseval/rvt021

Purinton, T., & Skaggs, J. (2017). *American universities abroad: The leadership of independent transnational higher education institutions*. American University in Cairo Press. ISBN 978 977 416 840 6.

Qureshi, S. S. (2008). Role of higher education in peace-building and strengthening national institutions. In *Proceedings of the 4th international Barcelona conference on higher education*, Barcelona. http://web.guni2005.upc.es/media/0000000500/0000000540.pdf

Sagy, S. (2002). Intergroup encounters between Jewish and Arab students in Israel: Towards an interactionist approach. *Intercultural Education*, *13*(3), 259–274. https://doi.org/10.1080/1467598022000008341

Tahirsylaj, A. (2008). Higher education in Kosovo: Major changes, reforms and development trends at University of Prishtina and University of Mitrovica and their role in peace building and reconciliation during post-conflict period. In *Proceedings of the 4th international Barcelona conference on higher education* (p. 5). http://www.guni-rmies.net

Temple, P. (2008). Learning spaces in higher education: An under-researched topic. *London Review of Education*, *6*(3), 229–241. https://doi.org/10.1080/14748460802489363

Tomovska, A. (2010). Contact as a tool for peace education? Reconsidering the contact hypothesis from the children's perspectives. *Journal of Peace Education*, *7*(2), 121–138. https://doi.org/10.1080/17400201.2010.498993

United Nations University. (2005). Call for world aid to repair Iraq's devastated universities. Retrieved November 17, 2023, from https://archive.unu.edu/update/archive/issue37_16.htm

Universities Canada. (n.d.). *Social impact*. Retrieved November 17, 2023, from https://www.univcan.ca/priorities/social-impact/

University of Michigan. (n.d.). *What is social impact?* Retrieved November 17, 2023, from https://businessimpact.umich.edu/about/what-is socialimpact/#:~:text=Definition%20of%20Social%20Impact,addresses%20a%20pressing%20ocial%20challenge

van der Wende, M. (2011). The emergence of liberal arts and sciences education in Europe: A comparative perspective. *Higher Education Policy*, *24*, 233–253. https://doi.org/10.1057/hep.2011.3

Wong, E. (2007, January 3). An American university for Iraq but not in Baghdad. *The New York Times*. Retrieved November 17, 2023, from https://www.nytimes.com/2007/01/03/world/middleeast/03university.html

Chapter 4

Leading the Policy Landscape of Somali Private Education System in a Conflict Zone: Views of Somali Headteachers

Krishan Sood and Abdishakur Tarah

Nottingham Trent University, UK

Abstract

The aim of this chapter is to understand the policy liberties and constraints within which school headteachers, and teachers aspire to promote high-quality education for their pupils in private schools in Somalia in the context of conflict in the country. This chapter develops this understanding of headteachers particularly in low-cost primary private schools in Somalia. The analysis in this chapter is informed by Mumford et al.'s Skills Model, as this approach combines the notion of knowledge and abilities necessary for effective leadership. First, using interview data with headteachers, we critique how headteachers in private schools in Mogadishu, Somalia, lead and manage schools when there is a crisis and conflict surrounding them, by unpacking the concepts of *leadership* and *management*. Second, we shed light on how well they are prepared and developed professionally to manage in such a turbulent environment caused by the war in Somalia. Here, we consider the role of the Federal Ministry of Education in the level of support that headteachers get in enacting their education policy. Third, this chapter discusses the impact of such crises on the quality of education provision for local private schools. Finally, this chapter identifies lessons to be learnt through suggested recommendations for headteachers in leading and managing education in times of turbulence and conflict. Here, we

---

Education and Sustainable Development in the Context of Crises:
International Case Studies of Transformational Change, 45–55
Copyright © 2025 by Krishan Sood and Abdishakur Tarah. Published by Emerald Publishing Limited. These works are published under the Creative Commons Attribution (CC BY 4.0) licence. Anyone may reproduce, distribute, translate and create derivative works of these works (for both commercial and non-commercial purposes), subject to full attribution to the original publication and authors. The full terms of this licence may be seen at http://creativecommons.org/licences/by/4.0/legalcode
doi:10.1108/978-1-83797-773-420241004

pose a suggestion for headteachers to consider if glocalisation, as a phenomenon, may offer a way to resolve local crises with local solutions in providing high-quality education for their students.

Keywords: Crises; private schools; headteachers; leadership development; education management

4.1 Introduction

The aim of this chapter is to understand how school leaders in Somali private schools lead high-quality education in the context of conflict in the country. Several researchers discuss the significant impact of armed conflict on the provision of education in some countries, like Somalia. A number of authors highlight the physical destruction of the education system, while others have looked at the extent to which these conflicts affect social development, human resources in education, and the emotional well-being of children in conflict (Tarah & Sood, 2022; Tooley & Longfield, 2017). Globally, of the 28.5 million primary school-aged children out of school in conflict-affected countries, 12.6 million live in sub-Saharan Africa, 5.3 million in South and West Asia, and 4 million in the Arab States. The vast majority, 95%, live in low- and lower-middle-income countries. Girls, who make up 55% of the total, are the worst affected, as they are often victims of rape and other sexual violence that accompanies armed conflicts (UNESCO, 2023).

There are many barriers faced by children living in armed conflict areas. These barriers include non-availability of schools in the worst-affected areas of a country, lack of recruitment of staff, or convincing former staff to return to teaching (Save the Children, 2013). The *Attacks on Education* published by Save the Children (2013) further explains that the quality of basic skills in children is 'diminished' due to poor resource availability in schools, leading to low attendance as the learning environment is not conducive. In such a difficult context then, it is understandable how and why these factors/barriers can lead to student drop-out, making the provision of high-quality education a major headteacher challenge.

4.2 Benadir Regional Administration

The research took place in Mogadishu, which is the main area of the Benadir Administration and is the capital city of Somalia. It has an estimated population of 1.6 million people which accounts for about 13% of the total population of Somalia, and it is the headquarters of the federal government and the small number of schools it manages (Education Sector Strategic Plan (ESSP), 2017). The city has the largest private primary and secondary schools in the country, and these are members of a large umbrella association. Despite the government restoring its role in the education sector, the position of umbrella associations remains strong, as important providers of education and guarantors of a minimal quality of education. Government data indicate that there are over 1,000 umbrella-affiliated schools in Somalia, providing education to over 250,000 students (MOECHE, 2017, p. 22). Unlike Puntland and Somaliland, the Benadir Regional Administration does not have its own education policy although it has recently been mandated to take over 23 public schools which were under the direct management of the MOECHE of the federal government. These schools were part of the Benadir Administration's initial statutory responsibilities with a view to subsequent progress.

4.3 Conceptualising Leadership

Gardner (1990, cited in Baker, 2014) defines leadership as an assembly of people for action, facilitated through persuasion. Since most leaders are also engaged in management, it is useful to distinguish between these two interrelated processes: leadership and management. Bush and Coleman (2000) think two terms are not synonymous, as 'one can be a leader without being a manager' (p. 18). Citing Bush and Coleman (2000, p. 19), Schon (1984) further explains that the doing of leadership can happen without 'the formal burdens of management' (p. 19).

A central element in many definitions of leadership is that there is a process of influence. Wasserberg (2002) claims leadership is more about unifying staff around key values. From his perspective as a secondary headteacher, he argues that these core values come down to: a) schools seen as centres of excellence in learning, and all members of the school community are learners; b) every member of the school community is valued as an individual; c) the school exists to serve its students and the local community; and d) learning is about the development of the whole person and happens in and out of classrooms.

In discussing the strategic dimension of leadership, West-Burnham and Harris (2015, p. 8) suggest three things that enable us to understand the strategic dimension of leadership: principle – the values informing an organisation's culture and priorities; purpose – the dominant view of the most important reason for the existence of the school; and people – their engagement, motivation, and performance in securing principles and purpose. They further suggest that the operational aspect of leadership, by contract, is about strategy and action, the management of doing.

Sood et al. (2018) note that in England, there are many good schools with good infrastructure and with adequate resources. This may not be the case in parts of Africa, like Somalia, which is the focus of this chapter, where headteachers are managing schools with little or no facilities/resources, untrained teachers, and students who are often hungry (Bush & Oduro, 2006). Under such a context, providing quality, sustainable education remains a challenge, and here, education holds the key to survival and remaining competitive (Wylie & Mitchell, 2003). There is no one model of 'doing' leadership or management in one or other way, it is context related, and in the Somalian context, the glocalised model of leadership may be more relevant and applicable. This allows headteachers in Somali schools to recognise and address how much inequality remains in education in the twenty-first century. It may be that inequality may be much greater in developing economies, due to the factors hinted at earlier, and the challenge for headteachers is how to manage socioeconomic divisions reproduced by education (Reay, 2010).

The headteachers in the private schools in Mogadishu are addressing such complex ideas, especially in the context of war crises, finite resources and little professional development or support for staff to lead and manage effectively; thus, each requires appropriate solutions in a localised manner. But slowly, headteachers are recognising the need to manage high-quality education provision drawing on the concepts of glocalisation – global issues, local actions (Robertson, 1992), with other authors preferring the term *globalisation* (Bottery, 2008; Mistry & Sood, 2012) which has resonance with reaching out to others as education is a global interest and concern for all. Such an opportunity for local actions is important in addressing issues of sustainable development in the climate of conflict.

4.4 School Leadership in a Conflict-Affected Environment

The enormity of the effects on education during and after armed conflict was felt everywhere. These effects included the complete destruction of education in both physical and human forms, and the voices of many frontline people were ignored (Pherali, 2016). There is a high prevalence of attacks on schools during armed conflict, with a commonality of deaths among pupils, teachers, and school leaders. Although there is an increasing literature that deals with relationships between education and armed personnel, there remains a gap in the literature on how to address the complex effects of trauma experienced by teachers and school leaders within the context of conflict and crisis of war (Pherali, 2016).

In their previous study on Somali headteachers' experience in operating in an active conflict environment, Tarah and Sood (2022) found despite community mobilisation to safely reopen schools, several school leaders face challenges in recovering school buildings for a safe return for children. Somali headteachers' experiences of the conflict in managing their schools, how they have faced violence and having to work in a challenging environment are further reported in Tarah and Sood (2022). One example was that of a school leader, who, with help from local communities and school staff, had to clear debris and dead bodies from school buildings before it was safe for students and staff. The staff removed 17 dead bodies from his school ground before the community had the trust to send their children there. These were not isolated cases but sadly, rather common ones. Another headteacher revealed that it took more than two years to negotiate with militiamen to vacate the school premises, and the deal on which they agreed to leave was a monthly share of 50% of the collected revenue.

Tarah and Sood (2022) also reported that headteachers experienced trauma and other psychological disturbances, with no support being available to them during those challenging times. Their study also found that school leaders were compelled to pay financial support to grieving families, even though the schools themselves were in financial difficulties. Waiting for unwelcome news of the death or injury of a member of staff or a student who was on the way to school was their daily expected briefing. Another effect of the conflict on schools was a shortage of teachers sometimes impelled school leaders to teach, especially those who possessed teaching skills. These turbulences impact on schools' overall subscriptions, as parents can remove their children if a school does not have sufficient teachers to teach them (Tarah & Sood, 2022).

As a result of the absence of government regulation and support, there are no institutions that prepare and develop headteachers in Somalia. Also, there is no formal training and leadership development for public and private primary headteachers in Somalia, whereas, in contrast, there is a growing recognition of the significance of school headship preparation through professional development and training across the world. Comparatively, the procedures used in appointing and offering pre-service training in many countries, particularly in Africa, are inadequate. Induction and in-service training for headteachers are also inappropriate in developing countries, especially those within the continent of Africa (Bush & Oduro, 2006). Globally, Kayiwa (2011) notes that headteachers do not receive training before taking up their post and often 'work from experience' (p. 1), which does not give confidence to the provision of education.

Although there are no specific Somalia-related studies on the availability of professional development opportunities for school leaders or a skills audit of current leaders of low-cost private schools in Somalia, the World Bank (2018) want them to have 'the required competencies and skills to lead, support, and challenge members of their institutions' (p. 72). It is important to acknowledge the link between the leadership competencies of school leaders and their positive impact on the success of schools (Davis et al., 2005, p. 3). In discussing this further in the context of school improvement and students' learning outcomes, it is important to acknowledge the relationship between different sections of schooling, including leadership and management. In addition to the role they play in improving students' achievements, they also lead on developing effective relationships among staff members, acquiring and allocating resources, promoting teacher development, improving student outcomes, and building mutually supportive school community relations.

At times of crises which school leaders and their staff are managing, their collective efficacy has to be considered as their psychological state may not be at its best. The staff have to talk about their feelings and experiences in a safe space, and this requires school headteachers to find time for tough conversations about teachers' self-efficacy and offer support in a school climate that is collaborative (DeWitt, 2017). Listening to staff voices helps in the process of mindfulness and building teachers' self-efficacy, motivation and belief in the process of collaborative trust building and willingness to share ideas.

According to a recent document published by the federal government of Somalia, one of the key components of its ESSP is the enhancement of the quality of education and children's learning outcomes through the provision of school-based coaching for headteachers to improve school performance (ESSP, 2017). To achieve this, it will develop comprehensive and consolidated headteacher training programmes. This strategy only applies to the education sector in Somalia (Benadir Region and Federal Member States), as Somaliland has its own ESSP. Although Somaliland's ESSP has extensive references to increasing female headteachers in Somaliland, there is nevertheless no mention of any direct government policy for preparing, developing, and training headteachers. The realities of school leadership in Somalia are complex. There are neither post-secondary educational headship programmes nor school-based apprenticeship programmes in Somalia. This makes it more difficult for school leaders to learn how to enact any type of leadership other than daily unavoidable managerial tasks (Khalifa et al., 2014, p. 236). Furthermore, it leaves headteachers untrained and with no professional development programmes available to them. We therefore need further study to understand the role of headteachers in post-conflict education in Somalia (World Bank, 2018, p. 72).

4.5 Methodology

It was important to collect the lived experiences of headteachers through a qualitative approach (Creswell, 2013). An approach advocated by Drever (1995), helped in refining our data collection involving sampling 30 private primary school headteachers in Somaliland, Puntland, and Banadir regions using a purposeful sampling method for interviews and observations, with 80 respondents completing the questionnaire. A select number of policy documents of the Somali Ministry of Education and international non-governmental organisations (NGOs), such as UNICEF, UNESCO, and the World Bank, were reviewed (Best & Kahn, 1993). Such triangulation allowed comparison of sources of evidence to determine the accuracy of information or phenomena (Cohen et al., 2018).

After data collection and data sorting, analysis was undertaken following Creswell's (2013) data analysis guide. Semi-structured interviews were conducted in the field as it allowed the exploration and sensitive probing of a series of specific questions or issues with the headteachers (Creswell, 2013). These were the headteachers who would provide the richest information and those who were the most interesting (Best & Kahn, 2006). We next present the findings based on Mumford's Skills Model: competencies and managing environmental changes.

4.6 Findings

Sixty percentage of those interviewed were headteachers before the civil war erupted. Of that 65%, 55% are currently in this role, while 10% have retired; 35% indicated that there were no headteachers before the armed conflict, and only 15% of this cohort were working in education, while 20% of this group were in education or school management. The vast majority of the participants serving as headteachers range in age from 36 to 60 years old. Over 80% serve more than 10 years as a headteacher, while 20% are in this role for more than six years.

In responding to the question regarding school operation during active armed conflict, only 20% stated that their schools were in operation at the start of the conflict, while 62% indicated that their schools were irregular in terms of operation due to school premises being occupied by armed militia or influential people who were not associated with any armed groups; 65% of the participants have indicated that they were headteachers during armed conflict, after successful reopening of their schools on an on-off basis due to ongoing conflict. In their responses to the negative impact on school operations, including staff and children's safety, recruiting teachers, and managing teaching and learning resources, participants indicated that their personal skills and experience played a significant role in the way they managed the effect of the conflict. Participants further explained the direct impact of the conflict on their role as headteachers and stated that these impacts include reopening of schools, concerns about safety to and from school for staff and children, safety during school time, teacher recruitment and retention, lack of means to manage staff performance and support, lack of resources, lack of support for teachers and other staff from outside the school, managing and maintaining external relations, and volatility of the situations and instabilities and lack of means to manage teaching and learning assessment.

In their responses to the question related to the strategies or managerial responses that participants undertook to minimise any impact of the armed conflict on their roles as headteachers, their responses varied, some were too generic and less detailed, while three provided detailed responses to the question. These are presented next for illustrative purpose:

Participant (HT06)

> My school was reopened as a result of community-led **mobilisation**, and this has enabled me to count on the **support** of the community. I led the school in **partnership** with the community and like-minded individuals. This was the best approach to managing the school during a crisis. Joint planning and organisational management with members of the community have enabled the management of the school to create a protected and **positive learning environment** for staff and children. **Personal qualities and competencies** have had a great influence on the way I applied this strategy.

Participant (HT09)

> I believe the **effective outcome of a leader** during a crisis is influenced by their **personal and professional skills** in dealing with challenges faced by the school. The skills include how you treat your staff, deal with significant issues, including safety and resources, and manage internal and external disputes. If teachers and staff are not happy, they will leave, and no teacher means no students. There is a **high demand for teachers,** pay, and safety in certain areas where conflict may still be active. **Shortages of teachers** sometimes force school leaders to teach, especially those who possess teaching skills. These **staff turbulences** have a knock-on effect on schools' overall subscription as **parents remove their children** if a school does not have any teachers to teach their children.

Participant (HT12)

> Every **school leader** must be **equipped with skills** that help him or her to **deal with people** who are experiencing many challenges

in life, including trauma and different personalities. The school leader must understand the circumstances surrounding the school during a crisis, including the armed conflict. Social skills, knowledge, and **spiritual competency** are vital skills for me and for others when it comes to being a leader. My personal experience during the armed conflict was that **staff faced repercussions** from parents and relatives of students if they failed or gave low marks to their children. In some cases, staff had to choose between life and death situations in assessing students, particularly those whose parents or relatives are part of the **militia group**. Communities will have greater respect for leaders who hold stronger spiritual competencies, compassion, and knowledge of education.

4.7 Discussion and Conclusion

The enormity of the effects on education during and after armed conflict was felt everywhere. The most affected were pupils who had disrupted education due to the armed conflict and constant threat of militia groups. This also impacted on parents as they were constantly worried about the safety and well-being of their children at school. The main priority for any parent or community during a crisis was the continuation of education. However noble this effort of reopening schools, this was not without a challenge. Most schools were not used for years during the conflict because they were in areas where armed conflict continued to be active. The consequence of conflict led to the complete destruction of education in both physical and human forms.

In responding to the question related to managing external environmental factors and their direct impact on education, few participants were explicit with their responses to the question. The headteacher's skills in dealing with these changes mattered significantly. They must have the ability to reconsider the operating systems that existed before the conflict and revisit these systems and their relevance to the changing environment. A considerable number of participants were headteachers before the civil war and felt the negative impact of the conflict immediately. Although participants' responses varied in strategies, they were used to continue providing education during armed conflict, and they strongly agreed that the conflict had a negative impact on schools' day-to-day operations.

There is unambiguous evidence that the headteachers' approaches to responding to external changes varied, and these were influenced by their skills, experience, and personal and professional competencies. These responses are linked with the statement by Mumford et al. (2000), who suggest that an effective performance by a headteacher during a crisis is determined by their capability and skills in problem-solving, social judgement skills, and knowledge. These skills included understanding and resolving complex problems (Northouse, 2016, p. 48). Defining these problems included how headteachers paid attention to these changes and their impact on school life and worked with others and communities to mobilise a collective response. Good social skills, knowledge, and spiritual competencies were vital when it came to collaborating with people from diverse groups, such as school staff, parents, and the wider community.

Participants also acknowledged that their key role as headteachers was to ensure that a normative environment was maintained, and effective relationships among staff members were maintained by acquiring and allocating resources, maintaining effective external relations, and building a mutually supportive school community. This is what Day and Sammons (2016) highlighted earlier, 'headteachers do this through building community leadership' (p. 7).

In conclusion, participants agreed with the notion that headteachers' successes in leading and managing schools during conflict depends on how they redefine culture and structure, resource management, the roles and responsibilities of staff, and their own, as well as managing external relations, which are vital in the case of armed conflict. Headteachers must gain the necessary competencies for effective 'karti', and these require a set of skills including personal and professional, cultural, and spiritual competencies, as well as experience and knowledge.

4.8 Recommendations

This chapter acknowledges the uniqueness of Somalia's education system, which has experienced total destruction for more than two decades. The enormity of the effects on education during and after armed conflict was felt everywhere, including in the teacher training provision as well as in the preparation and development of schools and school leaders. There is a proposal that headteachers are enacting policy through the concept of glocalisation, centred on local issues, local solutions, and in addition to providing high-quality education, they must remain focused on progressing ideas on international sustainable development. The authors make the following recommendations:

- Further research is needed on the impact of conflict on school management during conflict and what support is made available to them.
- There is a need for comprehensive education policies that guide all stakeholders in the provision of education services that support school headteachers.
- Training and development for school headteachers is imperative.
- School owners and the wider community support keeping children, staff, and school leaders safe during crises.
- For the headteachers, they create distributed leadership opportunities for middle managers. This helps middle leaders step in in the event of a headteacher absence.

References

Baker, E. L. (2014). Leadership and management – guiding principles, best practices, and core attributes. *Journal of Public Health Management and Practice, 20*(3), 356–357.
Best, J. W., & Kahn, J. V. (2006). *Research in Education* (10th edn.). Pearson.
Best, J., & Kahn, J. (1993). *Research in education* (8th edn.). Allyn.
Bottery, M. (2008). How different are we? Globalisation and the perceptions of leadership challenges in England and Hong Kong. *Educationalfutures, E-journal of the British Education Studies Association, 1*(1), 1–15.
Bush, T., & Coleman, M. (2000). *Leadership and strategic management in education*. Sage. https://doi.org/10.4135/9781446220320

Bush, T., & Oduro, G. (2006). New principals in Africa: Preparation, induction and practice. *Journal of Educational Administration, 44*(4), 359–375. https://doi.org/10.1108/09578230610676587

Cohen, L., Manion, L., & Morrison, K. (2018). *Research methods in education* (8th ed.). Routledge. ISBN 9781138209886.

Creswell, J. W. (2013). *Qualitative inquiry and research design.* Sage. ISBN 978-1-4129-9531-3.

Davis, S., Darling-Hammond, L., LaPointe, M., & Meyerson, D. (2005). *School leadership study: 'Developing successful principals'* (Review of Research). Stanford University, Stanford Educational Leadership Institute.

Day, C., Gu, Q., & Sammons, P. (2016). The impact of leadership on student outcomes: How successful school leaders use transformational and instructional strategies to make a difference. *Educational Administration Quarterly, 52*(2), 221–258. https://doi.org/10.1177/0013161X15616863

DeWitt, P. M. (2017). *School climate: Leading with collaborative efficacy.* Corwin. ISBN 9781506385990.

Drever, E. (1995). *Using semi-structured interviews in small-scale research. a teacher's guide.* Edinburgh, Scottish Council for Research in Education. ISBN-1-86003-011-4.

ESSP. (2017). *Education sector strategic plan 2018–2020.* Ministry of Education, Culture and Higher Education, Federal Government of Somalia.

Gardner, J. W. (1990). *On leadership.* The Free Press.

Kayiwa, B. (2011). *Assessment of leadership training of head teachers and secondary school performance in Mubende district, Uganda.* M.A. thesis, Bugema University, Kampala.

Khalifa, M. A., Bashir-Ali, K., Abdi, N., & Arnold, N. W. (2014). From post-colonial to new liberal schooling in Somalia: The need for cultural relevant school leadership among Somaliland principals. *Planning & Changing: An Educational Leadership and Policy Journal, 45*(3/4), 235–260.

Mistry, M., & Sood, K. (2012). How are leaders integrating the ideology of globalisation in primary school contexts? *Education 3-13: International Journal of Primary, Elementary and early Years Education, 1-13,* iFirst article. https://doi.org/10.1080/03004279.2011.609178

MoECHE. (2017). Education Sector Strategic Plan 2018-2020. Mogadishu, Ministry of Education, Culture and Higher Education, Federal Government of Somalia.

Mumford, M. D., Zaccaro, S. J., Harding, F. D., Jacobs, T. O., & Fleishman, E. A. (2000). Leadership skills for a changing world: Solving complex social problems. *Leadership Quarterly, 11*(1), 11–35. https://doi.org/10.1016/S1048-9843(99)00041-7

Northouse, P. G. (2016). *Leadership theory and practice.* Sage.

Pherali, T. (2016). School leadership during violent conflict: Rethinking education for peace in Nepal and beyond. *Comparative Education, 52*(4), 473–491.

Reay, D. (2010). Sociology, social class and education. In M. Apple, S. Ball, & L. A. Gandin (Eds.), *The Routledge handbook of the sociology of education* (396–404). Routledge. ISBN 0-203-86370-4.

Robertson, R. (1992). *Globalization: Social theory and global culture.* Sage. ISBN 9781446280447.

Save the Children. (2013). *Education under attack.* Save the Children.

Schon, D. A. (1984). Leadership as reflection-in-action. In T. Sergiovanni & J. Corbally (Eds.), *Leadership and organizational culture* (pp. 36–63). University of Illinois Press. ISBN 978-0-252-01347-8.

Sood, K., Peart, S., & Mistry, M. (2018). *Becoming a successful school leader- developing new insights.* Routledge. ISBN 978-1-138-1005-8.

Tarah, A., & Sood, K. (2022). Participatory action research: Challenges and opportunities of undertaking indigenous approach in examining school leadership in a conflict-affected zone. In M. F. Mbah, W. L. Filho, & S. Ajaps (Eds.), *Indigenous methodologies, research and practices for sustainable development. World sustainability series* (pp. 413–428). Springer. ISBN 9783031123252.

Tooley, J., & Longfield, D. (2017). *Education, war and peace: The surprising success of private schools in war-torn countries.* The Institute of Economic Affairs. ISBN 978-0-255-36747-9.

UNESCO. (2023). *Technology in education GEM report 2023.* UNESCO. https://www.unesco.org/gem-report/en

Wasserberg, M. (2002). *Creating the vision and making it happen.* Paul Chapman Publishing. ISBN 9781446265154.

West-Burnham, J., & Harris, D. (2015). *Leadership dialogues: Conversations and activities for leadership teams.* Crown House Publishing. ISBN 1845909062.

World Bank. (2018). *Study on understanding the role of non-state education providers in Somalia.* World Bank Group. https://doi.org/10.1596/31610

Wylie, C., & Mitchell, L. (2003, January). Sustaining school development in a decentralized system: Lessons from New Zealand. In *A paper presented at the International Congress for School Effectiveness and Improvement*, Sydney.

Chapter 5

Towards a Sustainable and Balanced Development of Higher Education in South Korea

Sang-Seok Moon[a] and Miriam Sang-Ah Park[b]

[a]Kangwon National University, South Korea
[b]Nottingham Trent University, UK

Abstract

Higher education institutions must keep up to date with the changing needs and situations of students, addressing societal issues affecting young people's lives and learning. Among the crises that higher education institutions in South Korea are facing, population decline and a lack of sustainable development present a significant threat to these institutions' existence as well as student satisfaction and learning experience. By relying on a review of relevant literature, this chapter will discuss each of these challenges and potential solutions. We hope that our discussion of the challenges in South Korea will also highlight that many of the 'crises' for higher education and ways to tackle them can be both localised and globally applicable. What is significant here is that higher education has a key role to play in preparing the young generation of Koreans to embrace sustainability and to foster resilience in them – for preparedness for future crises. We propose that a focus on community identity strength and education for sustainable development (ESD) can work as a solution for improving students' learning and global citizenship in these areas. Furthermore, we argue that this is especially important for preserving local and regional strengths and, ultimately, mutual development between the region and universities.

Education and Sustainable Development in the Context of Crises:
International Case Studies of Transformational Change, 57–69
Copyright © 2025 by Sang-Seok Moon and Miriam Sang-Ah Park. Published by Emerald Publishing Limited. These works are published under the Creative Commons Attribution (CC BY 4.0) licence. Anyone may reproduce, distribute, translate and create derivative works of these works (for both commercial and non-commercial purposes), subject to full attribution to the original publication and authors. The full terms of this licence may be seen at http://creativecommons.org/licences/by/4.0/legalcode
doi:10.1108/978-1-83797-773-420241005

Sustainable development depends on building a stronger and positive personal and collective identity, and students' active participation in sustainable development transcends the localised challenges. Such outcomes are also important for the sustainable future of higher education in South Korea and continuous development in the higher education scholarship.

Keywords: Higher education; South Korea; sustainable development goals (SDGs); environment, society, and governance (ESG); education for sustainable development (ESD)

5.1 Introduction

A 'crisis', both in the real-world scenario and in a higher education context, can take on various meanings and definitions. Whichever changes or circumstances that threaten the sustainability of any known ways of a higher education institution's existence or modus operandi can be considered a crisis. If one goes with this notion, a crisis is highly contextually dependent/variant, and the broader geopolitical context needs to be taken into account if one is to take on a global view of where higher education is located in the current times.

In South Korea, higher education institutions, particularly universities, are feeling the crisis at multiple levels (Ministry of Education (MoE), 2022). The decline in the school-age population is the first of them, which changes the demographics significantly and threatens the survival of some higher education institutions, especially outside of the capital and in the more rural regions. Since the 1980s, South Korea's fertility rate has steadily declined. In the process of industrialisation, the country has seen the previously large families turn into more nuclear families, and also with this trend, couples having less children overall. The birth rate, which was 4.74 in 1970, was 0.78 in 2022. This decline in the birth rate is also driven by the rising costs of raising children and of those in the middle and lower socioeconomic classes opting out of marriage and child rearing in turn (Ha, 2012; Kim et al., 2011, 2019).

On the contrary, the number of higher education institutions in South Korea has increased constantly, reaching 336 in 2021 nationally. There are currently 190 general universities, 134 junior colleges, 10 colleges of education, and 2 industrial colleges, despite the school-age population (6–21 years old) peaking at 14.4 million in 1980 and declining since (Kim, 2023). In 2023, this number is only 7.26 million, a decrease of 50.4% compared to 1980. By 2025, the situation will likely be even more severe, with the population expected to fall below 7 million and by 2030 only 5 million (Presidential Committee on Ageing Society and Population Policy (PCASPP), 2022). The other issue is that students tend to prefer attending universities in Seoul, the capital city, where there is a concentration of resources and jobs. As such, universities in other cities and towns struggle to deal with this double impact for their own survival as well as for ensuring relative value of education for their present and future students which, in turn, will sustain regional growth (Kim, 2023). Efforts to bridge this gap between Seoul/the capital city region and the rest of the country and to improve educational development opportunities in the smaller cities are much needed. Our chapter presents some suggestions which may help shape the future of higher education in the smaller cities in the country.

The decline in the school-age population is recognised as a national problem, not only specific to certain regions. Such a demographic change can easily be seen as a crisis that threatens the sustainable development of higher education institutions and not unlikely, their survival in the long run (Gangwon Regional Innovation Platform, 2023; MoE, 2023). Accordingly, the central government of South Korea has created a system to prepare universities for such challenges that are rising rapidly and promote sustainable development and environment, society, and governance (ESG) education that fits with the local characteristics. This means that universities, and especially universities outside of the capital city where sustainable development is even more key to regional growth and educational objectives, will need to act quickly to embrace such initiatives and re-think the value of education for their students (Mun & Yang, 2022).

ESD means that the central government educates the values, behaviours, and ways of life necessary for a sustainable development in a society at all levels of education in the midst of accelerated social changes following the COVID-19 pandemic. In addition, they are pushing to comply with the international norms of the organisation, ESG management being one of the key initiatives. Each education entity related to ESG and the sustainable development goals (SDGs) education in higher education is asked to demonstrate to what extent their projects have progressed against the tensions and challenges mentioned earlier.

Various policies have been proposed, such as the Regional Innovation Scheme (RIS) project and the Place, Problem, and Project (P3L) method. The region has become an important topic for universities and the Korean society in crisis as aforementioned (Gangwon Regional Innovation Platform, 2023). South Korea achieved economic growth and democratisation centred on the metropolitan area around the capital city. Localities or regions outside of this area tended to be recognised as a colony supplying human and material resources to the metropolitan area. However, as the crisis deepened, growth centred on the metropolitan area stagnated, and dispersion instead of concentration and regions instead of the metropolitan area began to be recognised as an important growth model (Moon, 2023a). With such a change, the status and role of the national universities naturally increase, and there are new opportunities for higher education institutions to be working closely with the region in which they are located. In South Korea, there are 10 national universities in each administrative region. The MoE, which is the central ministry, has asked local universities to promote the RIS project. RIS based on local government–university cooperation is recognised as a way for the country to cooperate with the region in the field of education to save the region and the university from the crises they are each faced with. Problem-based learning (PBL) has also been recognised as an effective substitute for the one-sided, instruction model previously quite dominant in Korean education and is spreading widely. Importantly, PBL seeks to strengthen local innovation capabilities by collaborating with the region in solving local problems with more practical solutions in mind.

In this chapter, the context of South Korea (which is sometimes also referred to as Korea) is in the spotlight. We will review relevant academic literature and policy documents to highlight the response of the Korean government and higher education institutions to two important recent crises (i.e., school-age population decline and the so-called regional decline more widely) and outline the process of recognising and coping with the challenges following and fuelled by the COVID-19 pandemic.

5.2 Higher Education in South Korea

5.2.1 Historical Background

In Korea, the central government or the state has traditionally had much power and influence on education. Through the Japanese Colonial Period and the Korean War, over-developed states were able to infiltrate civil society through centralised and efficient organisations and institutions, allowing the will of the state to penetrate civil society (Alavi, 1972). Education took root in this centralised system because citizens were educated in the way that aligned with the societal objectives to get through this challenging period and beyond (MoE, 1988). This strong state centrism is deeply entrenched in the society and education planning to this day (Moon, 2023a).

Therefore, one can expect that the definition of and proposed response to the crises as proposed by the government will have a huge impact on the higher education system's response and ensuing actions to cope with these crises in Korea. The government has strict guidelines and objectives for higher education that reflect on the societal goals. Curriculum review has led to the suggested inclusion of sustainable development and ESG-related content in 2015, and in 2022, glocalism featured as a hot topic and objective stressed by the government. Glocalism, a term that combines localisation and globalisation, has already been used as a political tool. Nevertheless, the newly found emphasis on this initiative rests heavily on the opportunity for the region to grow as an agent of globalisation rather than remaining on the periphery of the metropolitan area. In this sense, glocalism provides an important ideological direction for universities to permeate into the region (Moon, 2023a). Just as the American government tried to escape the threat of communism by developing the economies of Third World countries in the 1960s, the Korean government has the intention of reducing the burden on the central government by regional growths (Park, 2007).

The MoE in South Korea also periodically conducts university evaluations and provides government-funded projects. Under such guidelines and suggestions, national, public, and private universities are all required to follow the policies of the MoE carefully. MoE is always at the centre of the reform of the national system, deciding the direction of the development and changes in all higher education institutions. If any institution does not follow, it may face exclusion from future government support, and for this reason, it is sometimes criticised as a reincarnated Leviathan for higher education institutions (Sakong, 2017). More in-depth analysis of how, under such a hierarchical structure, universities are responding to the regional needs and sustaining growth is much needed.

5.2.2 COVID-19 and Its Impact on Higher Education Institutions in South Korea

COVID-19 has also had a huge impact on higher education in Korea as would have been the case globally. There are, for instance, studies in areas where various crises caused by the transition to non-face-to-face teaching methods and digital transformation due to COVID-19 have been applied to education, threatening the sustainability of higher education (Crawford & Cifuentes-Faura, 2022). The rapid transformation in the main delivery mode of teaching and student expectations will inevitably lead to further impact on education that will have to be looked at carefully.

Education institutions are also faced with a major change as the result of the increased focus on the region as the centre as a solution, namely, more region-focused developments, in order to cope with the challenges brought on or accelerated by the pandemic. In an environment where the topic of SDGs and ESG management is spreading around the world, Korea has begun to respond actively to these global trends. As institutions of higher education emerged as a solution to the crisis in the region, various programmes focusing on regional cooperation, regional education and governance within the region emerged. Since 2015, the government revamped the curriculum to encourage elementary, secondary and high school students to learn and experience contents relating to sustainable development while keeping up with the trend of globalisation. In particular, education on the environment and sustainable development was included in the revised curriculum, and the government under President Moon Jae-In set strengthening sustainable development as a national task in 2018. The government sought to establish and strongly promote the Korean sustainable development goals (K-SDGs) that complement the '3rd Basic Plan for Sustainable Development'. Accordingly, by 2023, all local governments and institutions of higher education are required to develop a master plan and action plan and report it to the prime minister's office every year (Lee, 2023).

5.2.3 SDGs and ESG Management

Currently, research on SDGs and ESG in South Korea generally focuses on two dimensions: whether the SDGs are included in the curriculum within universities and how they might be implemented and linked to the regional goals. Accordingly, each educational entity continues to develop programmes within the curriculum, within the school, between schools and in conjunction with schools and other civic and social and community organisations (Kim, 2023). Naturally, research related to ESD and ESG management generally places emphasis on structural reforms and related roles within universities. However, sustainability research at universities has not yet progressed beyond the level of reporting on such data and we argue that more in-depth research and analysis is needed. First of all, it is important that we understand how the SDGs are being implemented within universities. Lee (2020) argues that universities should think about how to innovate and practice education and expand their role in the society. In other words, we need to learn how we can make students understand sustainable development and think about implementing them in their daily lives (Choi & Ji, 2023; Lee, 2023). There have been initiatives to engage with such goals, such as providing liberal arts education at universities as a way of educating students of their role in sustainable development. For instance, the Korean MoE's Glocal University 30 project encompassing the existing university education innovation project and regional linkage project is underway, although the success of this project has yet to be seen with little research tracing its impact so far. Unlike in Korea, sustainability and ESG concepts have been introduced in higher education for quite some time in Europe. Even in such countries, however, the majority of the research looks only at sustainability concepts and quality assurance in higher education (Manatos et al., 2017) and thus focusing on the delivery but not so much the impact and implications of such programmes on students or local contexts.

According to press releases, many universities in Korea have set up internal groups such as ESG committees, in order to facilitate ESG management. The establishment of ESG-related institutions is of great significance in that it serves as a practical starting point for ESG management. Konkuk University in Seoul led on such developments. In April 2021, they established the 'ESG Committee' under the direct supervision of the chairman of the board of directors of the school corporation and enhanced its expertise by establishing three divisions under the committee: environment, social responsibility and transparent management (Lee, 2023). Their ESG committee prepares practical strategies and measures for efforts to reduce carbon emissions, introduce eco-friendly energy and strengthen social responsibilities such as employment, safety, human rights and youth entrepreneurship for various stakeholders, ethical management and transparency (Cho, 2021). Korea University also established their ESG committee in April 2021 with the aim of making the SDGs a core value of the university management and actively fulfilling its social responsibility in applying ESG values to university education, research and administration (Song, 2022). Other universities including Seoul National University and Keonyang University followed suit in establishing ESG committees and research institutes in the following years to serve the purpose of strengthening environmental, climate and ethical education and operating comparative and course ESG programmes among others. Chung-Ang University launched the '2030 Carbon Neutral ESG Sharing Forum' with the participation of top experts in Korea with the goal of advancing carbon neutrality from 2050 to 2030 and leading ESG-related industries (Choi, 2021). The main aim of these establishments and new initiatives all link to establishing a strong ESG linkage system by bringing together industry, academia, and research networks and minimising the cost of building supply chain management (SCM) for each industry.

5.2.3.1 ESG Management of Universities

In South Korea, a university is an organisation consisting of hundreds of faculty members and thousands of students. As such, it has the character of a community-based enterprise in terms of economic activities such as job creation, service provision, and consumption. At the same time, it is also a public institution in that it provides educational services publicly and receives financial support from the state. Therefore, universities, like companies and public institutions, should conduct their own ESG management for sustainable development and should take the lead in spreading ESG culture to all parts of society. As we have seen, many universities in Korea have already established ESG committees, declared ESG visions, and set detailed implementation tasks. However, compared to major universities, companies, and public institutions overseas, there is still a lack of awareness and practice of ESG management across higher education institutions in Korea, and there is almost no disclosure of ESG-related information or socially responsible investing (SRI).

5.2.3.2 Operation of ESG Committee and Efforts to Spread ESG Culture

Experts have noted that ESG management in Korean higher education institutions is still only at a beginning stage (Kim, 2022a). In order to have effective ESG management in universities, the ESG committee should have autonomous control over its ESG management. The ESG committee should establish governance in which various involved actors such as faculty, staff, students, and alumni associations participate to discuss agendas and share achievements from time to time, and the ESG committee should be able to coordinate activities and establish priorities by exerting leadership (Kim, 2022). As there can be a conflict of interest between various departments of the university or various stakeholders of the university, there must be an organisation that has the authority to coordinate and prioritise the direction of the university, its budgeting, and resource allocation.

In addition, ESG management must include considerations for all stakeholders involved, including the socially disadvantaged, awareness of the rights and safety of all members and suppliers, and democratic and fair management. Some ways to spread the ESG culture created at universities include education, service, and community engagement (Leem, 2022). In addition to education for university students and professionals, eco-friendly ecological education and green consumption education should also be conducted for community members. In addition, it is necessary to systematically carry out social service activities within the broad framework of ESG. For example, Korea University's Social Contribution Centre has an ESG committee within the institution, which conducts continuous and systematic volunteer activities for underprivileged areas, people with disabilities, multicultural/North Korean defectors, the elderly living alone, and children/adolescents (Korea University Social Service Organisation, 2022). In addition, it is necessary for universities to take the lead in consulting for ESG management by public institutions and companies in the local community and for university professors to actively participate as ESG committee members of public institutions or companies.

5.2.3.3 Disclosure and Dissemination of ESG Information By Universities

Dissemination of information by universities through the publication of sustainability reports is another way in which the sharing and transfer of knowledge can occur at the local and national levels. Since 2019, Seoul National University's sustainability institute has prepared a sustainability report in compliance with the guidelines of the Global Reporting Initiative (GRI) for ESG and published it after being verified by an external party and has been publishing a green report every year since 2014 to share information related to the university's green campus activities and greenhouse gases related to each campus and major buildings (Seoul National University Institute for Sustainable Development, 2021). Yonsei University established the 'Global Social Contribution Institute' in 2017 to declare social participation as the central responsibility of the university. They are taking the lead in achieving the UN's SDGs through various activities and have prepared and published a sustainability report every year since 2020. In addition, Hanyang University, Aju University, and Wonkwang University are also publishing sustainability reports detailing their involvement and steps towards a sustainable future (Kim, 2022).

However, ESG information disclosure at universities is not mandatory at present, and there are no disclosure standards. Therefore, most universities do not disclose ESG information, and even universities that disclose ESG-related information adhere only to various standards set by themselves. In addition, disclosure methods vary, and some sustainability reports are difficult to locate. Therefore, it is necessary to develop ESG guidelines and evaluation indicators to be applied across institutions. The Korean MoE could help create and provide ESG guidelines, but it would be preferable to make them university led (Ministry of Trade, Industry and Energy (MTIE), 2021; Park & Jeong, 2021). It is true that universities need ESG and have an obligation to practise it, but if the MoE provides ESG guidelines to be applied to universities and applies them uniformly, there is a risk that ESG will turn into another university evaluation standard. In addition, it would be better to make ESG-related disclosures through university alerts rather than disclosing them separately on the university website or the websites of related institutions within it (Korea Foundation for the Advancement of History, 2022).

5.2.3.4 ESG University Cluster

The 2023 ESG University Cluster Agreement Ceremony and Forum was held, attended by 32 universities nationwide under the theme of 'Drawing the Future of Growth, Sustainability, and Sustainability of Universities with ESG'. The ESG University Cluster has declared that it will set and implement five common goals based on the ideology of ESG, such as taking the lead in environmental protection by creating a eco-friendly campus for the sustainable development of universities, creating social values for the realisation of an inclusive and safe society, and establishing transparent and fair governance. Initiatives including an ESG club where students and faculty members at each university can work together to promote ESG while using the platform created by the 'Korea ESG Management Institute' are proposed.

5.2.4 Regional Cooperations Between Universities and Local Government

Universities, local governments, and companies are cooperating in ESG management for the common goal of revitalising the local economy and awareness of the crisis caused by the decline in the school-age population. ESG is not just a corporate issue but a social issue, and universities, which sit at the centre of research and education, can practise ESG management through cooperation with local communities (local governments, public institutions, industries, etc.). In November 2021, Chungnam National University launched the ESG Promotion Council with the participation of universities, local governments, public institutions, industries, and research institutes such as Chungcheongnam Province, Daejeon City, Sejong City, Startup Promotion Agency, and Hyundai Jeongju with the purpose of laying the foundation for a regional innovation system (Lee, 2023).

To this end, it has placed the emphasis on the role of education in building local value chains and plans to hold an ESG social value academy for professional development. Handong University, in cooperation with three organisations including Pohang City and the Korean Council of UNAI KOREA, has decided to implement Global Citizenship Education from March 2022 for sustainable development through financial support from Pohang City and the utilisation of Handong University's teaching resources. Likewise, six universities in the Jeonbuk region (Jeonbuk National University, Jeonju National University, Jeonju National University of Education, Jesus University, Jeonju Jeonju University, and Jeonju Vision University) signed the 'Jeonju-University ESG Agreement' with Jeonju City to realise ESG values (Lee, 2022). In 2021, Inha University collaborated with four public companies in the Incheon area (Metropolitan Landfill Management Corporation, Incheon International Airport Corporation, Korea Environment Corporation, and Incheon Transportation Corporation) to hold a student contest to propose ESG management innovation ideas to these public companies. In September 2022, the Incheon University LINC 3.0 Project Group was established by the Incheon Port Corporation, under a business agreement with the Metropolitan Landfill Management Corporation and the Incheon Transportation Corporation for cooperation in the ESG Management Innovation Idea Contest and plans to select and award excellent work through student competitions (Kim, 2022). In November 2022, 120 students from 12 universities, including Hanseo University, Chung-Ang University, and Chosun University, who are carrying out the LINC3.0 project, participated in a project to develop ESG ideas for companies in Taean, South Chungcheong Province (Song, 2022).

5.2.5 Change in Participation and Perception

As Bandura's (1982) concept of self-efficacy suggests, active participation and especially participating in activities that directly relate to one's goals has a profound impact on the individual(s) involved. When university students participate in programmes co-created by the state and universities in response to national policies for survival and growth, they are much more likely to see its direct potential outcomes and find stronger motivation to take part and bring about the intended desired outcome. This could also lead to students getting a broader and better understanding of the local region and affect their sense of citizenship and belonging which in turn can transform them into participatory citizens. This can also take them out of their shell, worrying only of their personal achievements and anxiety to catch up with the developments within the capital city, and establish a more grounded identity as someone who belongs and works for the growth of the locality. A young businessman having set up a social enterprise together with his college mate in Chuncheon speaks of his experience which closely follows this, noting that he has managed to combine his vision with that of the city, Chuncheon, and that it has been a satisfactory journey (Moon, 2023b).

The emergence of the RIS project, mentioned earlier, which combines the visions of university innovation and regional innovation, has led many national universities in smaller cities to identify ways to utilise national resources optimally. As an example, universities in Gangwon province have implemented programmes to encourage local residents and youth to solve problems in their local region (Gangwon Regional Innovation Platform, 2023). The mission of many such universities outside of Seoul in the coming years is to carry out more of such projects, have a closer focus on the regional needs and engage students and staff to work on these needs and eventually, and contribute to regional growth by attracting and keeping talented young people who will stay and continue to work towards these goals locally. In this sense, university research and education for their students, who are local youth, can aim to improve their understanding of the region and become experts in the region. Making them region focused may be the best solution to balancing outgrowth across regions, and such a strategy fits the age of glocalisation well.

At Kangwon National University, there is a new project called 'Students Club Research Projects', a student community club which focuses on young people establishing themselves in Chuncheon, the city in which the university is located (Gangwon Regional Innovation Platform, 2023). Students who join this club try to engage with local issues and identify opportunities to find solutions to these issues while turning them into career opportunities for themselves. Students are invited to participate in competitions run by the Centre for Innovation in Higher Education with staff mentors, and the aim is to get students involved in these projects where they can form social capital with a wide range of people in the region, including fellow students with similar goals as well as public institutions and local residents. Also, through these projects, students learn to identify an issue and form and conduct autonomous research under the guidance of academic staff, and in this sense, it fulfils the educational purpose in training students to think independently and critically. The government has promised substantial funding to support these programmes for the coming years, and universities are keen to be selected to be funded for these programmes and also come up with ways to engage students effectively. Another added benefit to such programmes is that this provides the best opportunity to open up the campus for discussions across various stakeholders, inviting local residents and activists to have open and progressive conversations with the universities and their students to work on local issues together. We hope that this will lead to more integrated local systems of communities and universities working together that serve as an open space for research and community work for all.

5.3 Discussion and Conclusion

Population decline, along with centralisation of resources and opportunities in the capital city, has led to challenges for smaller cities and higher education institutions in the regions in attracting young people to study and stay in their cities. Also, the socioeconomic changes brought on by the COVID-19 pandemic have led to an alarming sense of crisis felt and experienced by higher education institutions in South Korea. The state-centred management of educational institutions and national agenda have traditionally impacted on the universities' ability and scope to make autonomous decisions and create policies and programmes that serve themselves and their students best. We propose that closer cooperation between higher education institutions, local governments, and stakeholders are needed, with the students playing the role of active agents serving as a linkage point between. Such an opportunity will also allow students to consider a wider range of options for their academic and career pathways as the result of their involvement in these projects, local knowledge, and social capital.

The current crises have also served as a wake-up call at the national level, leading to the realisation and consensus that more attention needs to be paid to the local needs and how universities in each region and city can better reflect these needs alongside their students' needs. A variety of new programmes and projects that closely align with regional issues has been introduced, which centre around higher education institutions acting as the regional hub. As outlined in our chapter, many of these programmes and projects focus on sustainable development at local and national levels and universities are keen to involve students in these, so that they can develop a better awareness and understanding of the local needs while gaining first-hand experience in PBL and research focused on generating practical and locally applicable solutions. We would like to argue that such endeavours will help higher education institutions to manage wisely with the present challenges and, furthermore, serve the students and communities more optimally in the coming years.

References

Alavi, H. (1972). The state in post-colonial societies: Pakistan and Bangladesh. *New Left Review, 74*(4), 59–81.
Bandura, A. (1982). Self-efficacy mechanism in human agency. *American Psychologist, 37*(2), 122. https://psycnet.apa.org/doi/10.1037/0003-066X.37.2.122
Cho, H. (2021, September 3). *Education ESG 'turning crisis into opportunity: University Town takes steps to introduce ESG'*. Aju Economics.
Choi, J. (2021, November 27). *Chung-Ang University launched the 2030 carbon neutral ESG sharing forum*. Maeil.

Choi, J., & Ji, Y. (2023). A study on sustainable regional cooperation through the implementation of SDGs in universities. *The Journal of Humanities and Social Science, 14*(3), 4209–4224.

Crawford, J., & Cifuentes-Faura, J. (2022). Sustainability in higher education during the COVID-19 pandemic: A systematic review. *Sustainability, 14*, 1879. https://doi.org/10.3390/su14031879

Gangwon Regional Innovation Platform. (2023, January 18). *Gangwon LRS sharing university convergence major innovative talent announcement.* https://www.gwplatform.or.kr/

Ha, J. (2012). An economic analysis of low fertility in Korea: Focusing on income inequality and cost of education. *The Review of Social & Economic Studies, 39*, 137–174.

Kim, C. (2022a, May 22). Seoul National University takes the first step toward ESG. *Taehaksinbo.*

Kim, E. B. (2023). Changes and alternatives in education due to decline in school-age population. *Seoul Education Special Edition, 6S*(3).

Kim, E., Lee, S., Lee, W., Kim, H. (2011). *Study on the fertility and child care behaviour by income group and policy directions.* Research Report of Korea Institute for Health and Social Affairs (KHIASA), 2011-37-4.

Kim, E. B., You, S. C., Park, K. B., Baek, Y. S., Park, S. M., (2019). Tasks for the future education of elementary schools in the face of a decrease in the population. *Journal of Competency Development & Learning, 14*(3), 193–221.

Kim, H. (2022b, November 22). University EGS into capital market. *E-today.*

Korea Foundation for the Advancement of History. (2022). *2020–2021 Korea Foundation for the Advancement of History sustainable management report.*

Korea University Social Service Organisation. (2022). *KUSSO 14.* Korea University, ibook.

Lee, C. (2020). A study on the innovation of university education and the improvement of social role of university through SDGS. *Korean Comparative Government Review, 24*(2), 123–148.

Lee, C. (2023). Research on the relationship and responsibility between the humanities and social sciences and science and technology fields for university SDGs/ESG implementation. *Humanitas Forum, 9*(2), 9–49.

Lee, J. (2022, January 21). University's 'ESG management' expanded to local governments … Examples of cooperation everywhere. *Hankookdaehakshinmun.*

Leem, T. (2022). ESG fever at universities and the role of universities. *The Korean Society of Management Consulting, 22*(6), 355–356.

Manatos, M., Sarrico, C. S., & Rosa, M. (2017). The integration of quality management in higher education institutions: A systematic literature review. *Total Quality Management & Business Excellence, 13*(1–2), 159–175.

Ministry of Education (MoE). (1988). *50 Years history of Korean education.*

Ministry of Education (MoE). (2022). *Korean education statistics service.*

Ministry of Education (MoE). (2023). *Glocal30 project briefing.*

Ministry of Trade, Industry and Energy (MTIE). (2021). *K-ESG guideline V1.0.*

Moon, S. (2023a). Sustainability development and glocalization: Towards globalization of local based networks. *Society and Theory, 44*, 235–276.

Moon, S. (2023b). Sustainable development and community. Network, platform: Chuncheon youth awareness. *Korean Regional Sociology, 24*(1), 59–88.

Mun, J., & Yang, C. (2022). Research trend analysis on education and sustainability. *Asian Journal of Education, 23*(3), 557–585.

Park, T., & Jeong, S. (2021). The effect of education for sustainable development on higher education. *The Korean Society of Culture and Convergence, 43*(1), 73–94.

Park, T. G. (2007). *Archetype and metamorphosis: The origin of Korea's economic development plans.* Seoul Taehakkyo Chulpanbu.

Presidential Committee on Ageing Society and Population Policy (PCASPP). (2022). *Changes in demographic structure and government response plan.*
Sakong, Y. (2017). Reincarnated Leviathan: A critic of the university assessment policy. *The Korea Association for Policy Studies, 26*(4), 163–196.
Seoul National University Institute for Sustainable Development. (2021). *Seoul National University Sustainability report and green report.*
Song, H. S. (2022). A study on the feasibility of SDGs in university liberal arts education. *The Journal of General Education, 15,* 199–228.

Part III

Chapter 6

Migration in Education Research: A Synthesis to Support Sustainable Development

F. Sehkar Fayda-Kinik[a] and Aylin Kirisci-Sarikaya[b]

[a]Istanbul Technical University, Turkey
[b]Izmir Democracy University, Turkey

Abstract

Migration has become a challenging issue in the field of education and an ongoing crisis for many countries. The migration crisis and education have a reciprocal relationship in that the influx of migrants puts a strain on educational systems, particularly regarding resources, funding, and linguistic and cultural differences. However, education can play a crucial role in addressing some of the challenges associated with migration, such as the need to integrate, skill acquisition and cultural awareness in host countries, as well as brain drain in the countries of origin. It is crucial to investigate how education can both address the problems caused by migration and maximise its potential for sustainable development. This chapter targets analysing relevant scholarship and aims to illustrate the broad patterns of relevant scholarly sources on migration in the field of education indexed in the Web of Science between 2015 and 2022, explore their collaboration trends, and reveal the conceptual structure of these studies in the context of international sustainable development. A bibliometric methodology is employed for the exploration and analysis of the publications; 991 studies on migration in the field of education are descriptively analysed in terms of distribution of publications with their citations, topics at the micro

---

Education and Sustainable Development in the Context of Crises:
International Case Studies of Transformational Change, 73–106
Copyright © 2025 by F. Sehkar Fayda-Kinik and Aylin Kirisci-Sarikaya. Published by Emerald Publishing Limited. These works are published under the Creative Commons Attribution (CC BY 4.0) licence. Anyone may reproduce, distribute, translate and create derivative works of these works (for both commercial and non-commercial purposes), subject to full attribution to the original publication and authors. The full terms of this licence may be seen at http://creativecommons.org/licences/by/4.0/legalcode
doi:10.1108/978-1-83797-773-420241006

level, journals, and the number of authors contributing to these papers. The results contribute to picturing the characteristics and collaboration trend of the scholarly sources on migration in the area of education as a challenging disabler or a driving force that contributes to societal development within the scope of international sustainable development.

Keywords: Migration; educational research; sustainable development; bibliometric analysis; scholarly analysis

6.1. Introduction

Migration, in its diverse forms and complexities, has emerged as a prominent and intricate global phenomenon that transcends geographical, social, and cultural boundaries. Its multifaceted impact spans across various sectors including education, which is a significant arena that is profoundly affected by the waves of human movement. Migration has recently taken a central stage on the international agenda, presenting opportunities and challenges for societies all over the world (Mosler Vidal & Laczko, 2022). Migration and education are intertwined in many aspects; moreover, education and skills development are significant factors at many points during an individual's migration mainly driven by differences in skills returns between the country of origin and the country of destination (Dustmann & Glitz, 2011). Further, historical analyses on migration emphasise how skills and education levels have played pivotal roles in shaping migration patterns across different periods by providing insights into the complex relationship between migration and the accumulation of human capital (Bernard & Bell, 2018; Bilecen, 2020; Hatton & Williamson, 1998). As a result, a symbiotic relationship has developed that is essential in determining how individuals and societies will develop in an increasingly globalised world.

The modern era has been witnessing an unprecedented surge in international migration, with the number of migrants reaching approximately 281 million worldwide, constituting about 3.6% of the global population (International Organization for Migration (IOM), 2022). This influx of migrants presents complex challenges to host countries' educational systems, exerting pressures on resources, funding, and the accommodation of linguistic and cultural diversity (Arjona-Pelado & Atnashev, 2021). Simultaneously, the field of education emerges as a dynamic force capable of addressing the complexities presented by migration, offering solutions to integration, skills acquisition, cultural awareness, and knowledge transfer, which are essential for both migrants and host communities. In achieving the sustainable development goals (SDGs) by 2030, English and Mayo (2021) emphasised the importance of lifelong learning by expanding SDGs to include the support and empowerment of migrant populations. Because of the dynamic relationship between migration and education, it is important to investigate how education can both address the problems caused by migration and maximise its potential for sustainable development.

Migration is more than a demographic shift that embodies a socio-political phenomenon inextricably intertwined with broader socio-economic structures. The challenges brought by migration span beyond the immediate domain of the educational sector and affect various aspects of society such as labour markets, healthcare systems, and cultural integration (Suárez-Orozco et al., 2009). Consequently, the multifaceted nature of migration necessitates a holistic understanding that considers not only the challenges but also the transformative opportunities it offers, particularly through the lens of education. As the world struggles to understand the complexities of migration and its implications, the context of sustainable development emerges as a critical framework to assess the implications of human mobility. Sustainable development entails the balanced pursuit of economic growth, social inclusion, and environmental preservation. Migration patterns can lead to resource distribution imbalances, thereby influencing access to quality education and skills development, which are crucial for achieving SDGs (United Nations Educational, Scientific and Cultural Organization (UNESCO), 2020). In this respect, migration plays a defining role in shaping the outcomes of these objectives and education contributes to sustainable development to overcome the challenges resulting from migration (Arjona-Pelado & Atnashev, 2021; English & Mayo, 2021).

Within this context, educational research has the unique responsibility of unravelling the multifaceted dimensions of migration and its impacts on societies. Scholars in the field have been actively examining the reciprocal relationship between migration and education, exploring ways in which education can serve as a catalyst for positive outcomes amid the complexities of migration (Rao, 2010; Suárez-Orozco & Qin-Hilliard, 2004). Therefore, this chapter sought to navigate the intricate landscape of migration in educational research, particularly in the context of international sustainable development. By conducting a comprehensive bibliometric analysis of the scholarly sources indexed in the Web of Science (WOS) between 2015 and 2022, this chapter aimed to shed light on the characteristics, collaboration trends, and conceptual structure of migration studies within the realm of education. Through this analysis, it was targeted to decipher the contribution of educational research to the discourse on migration and international sustainable development.

6.2. Conceptual Considerations and Literature Review

6.2.1. Migration in Education

Due to its profound implications for individuals, societies, and economies worldwide, the intersection of migration and education has captured significant scholarly attention. Migration can be defined as the movement of people across national or geographical boundaries (Rees, 2009). It encompasses various forms such as 'the movement of people across national borders' called international migration, 'the movement of people within a country' considered as internal migration, and 'the movement of people who are compelled to leave their homes due to conflict, persecution, or natural disasters' termed as forced migration

(Skeldon, 2018). According to the IOM (2023), any individual who moves across an international border or within a nation's borders away from his or her typical place of residence is considered a migrant, regardless of the following factors such as the legal status of the individual, whether the movement is voluntary or involuntary, the reasons for the movement, and the duration individuals spend living or staying in a particular location.

Within the context of education, migration involves the mobility of individuals or families seeking educational opportunities in different regions or countries, leading to a diversity of student populations in educational institutions. Education and migration have a significant relationship because it affects social disadvantage, labour migration, and intergenerational social mobility (Bilecen, 2020). Education systems play a significant role in reproducing social inequality based on social class, gender, and minority ethnicity; in addition, migration and international mobility shape an individual's possibilities in education (Chamakalayil & Riegel, 2016; Jacobs, 2022; Olowookere et al., 2022). Migration is integral to human development and enhances educational outcomes, with internal migration supporting the economy and increasing human capital in certain regions (Bernard & Bell, 2018). Therefore, the field of migration, academic mobility, and education has gained interest in international and comparative education, exploring the educational experiences and challenges different migrant groups have had, which can be used for educational practice and policies (Arnot et al., 2023).

The complex relationship between migration and education has been investigated from multiple perspectives. The influx of migrant students results in demands on educational systems, which necessitates considerations for linguistic and cultural diversity, equitable access to educational resources, and strategies for social integration (Benson, 2019; Organisation for Economic Co-operation and Development (OECD), 2018). On the other hand, education serves as a vehicle for the enhancement of the social and economic integration of migrants into host societies. It also plays a vital role in skills development, cultural adaptation, and intercultural understanding (Martini, 2021; Suárez-Orozco et al., 2010). Furthermore, it is often linked to the notion of 'social capital' because educational attainment can facilitate social mobility and enhance migrants' overall well-being (du Plooy et al., 2020, p. 2).

The impact of migration on education is not limited to host countries, and it also has some implications for countries of origin. The phenomenon of 'brain drain' occurs when highly skilled individuals migrate to pursue educational and career opportunities abroad, which potentially leads to the loss of human capital and expertise in the home country; conversely, 'brain gain' occurs when the return of skilled migrants contributes to knowledge transfer and capacity-building in their home countries (Gomellini & Ó Gráda, 2019, p. 168). The interconnectedness of migration and education underscores the importance of understanding the dynamics, challenges, and opportunities presented by these phenomena in order to formulate effective policies and strategies that promote inclusive and equitable education for all (UNESCO, 2020).

6.2.2. Educational Migration for Sustainable Development

Sustainable development, which first emerged as an economic concept, has evolved and deepened in meaning over time. The term 'sustainable development' first attracted attention in the *Our Common Future* report, also known as the Brundtland Report of the United Nations (UN), in 1987, and it was defined as 'development that meets the needs of the present without compromising the ability of future generations to meet their own needs' (The World Commission on Environment and Development (WCED), 1987). This prominent definition still serves as a guide for professionals working on this subject today, and it encompasses the broad idea of the goals of worldwide social advancement, economic growth, and environmental protection. International sustainable development can only be feasible when these three core objectives are supported by and coexist with one another (UN, 2023).

A significant milestone in the history of sustainable development, the millennium development goals (MDGs), composed of eight goals primarily aimed at developing countries, developed by the UN Millennium Summit in 2000 and officially launched in 2001. A new set of goals, the 17 SDGs of the UN Agenda 2030, were officially recognised by UN member states in 2015 to continue the progress started by the MDGs and fall inside the framework for global development by 2030. Countries have been incorporating the SDGs into their national policies in an effort to promote sustainable development; however, from time to time, various events or crises hinder or accelerate the move. The sustainable development agenda, for instance, is at risk due to some security, climate-dependent, or health concerns – the Covid-19 pandemic severely harmed sustainable progress everywhere (Sachs et al., 2022). Amid these crises, humanity's 'capacities to navigate uncertain futures' (United Nations Development Programme (UNDP), 2022); in other words, sustainable development which offers a road map to overcome the problems should be supported and preserved.

The 2030 Agenda for Sustainable Development, for the first time, stresses dedication to the migration issue as an international concern in its objectives. The inclusion and commitment that 'no one will be left behind' are emphasised as a fundamental tenet of the Agenda 2030, and the significance of migration is highlighted as a factor that can lead to both development and alleviation of poverty (United Nations General Assembly, 2015). In the context of migration and the achievement of SDGs, lifelong learning which encompasses learning practices of all age groups, at all education levels, in all learning contexts, as well as via a number of modalities (UNESCO Institute for Lifelong Learning (UIL), 2023) plays a critical role in meeting an array of learning needs and expectations. To be more detailed and give some examples in terms of the contribution of lifelong learning in the quest for migrants' right to live a dignified life and have decent work (UN, 2023), which serves as the cornerstone of SDGs, it could facilitate social cohesion by contributing to peaceful and inclusive societies (SDG 16), promote decent work and economic growth (SDG 8), increase educational opportunities for migrant women by empowering them economically and socially (SDG 5), and reduce inequalities (SDG 10).

When it comes to educational migration or international students, there is a phenomenon when individuals pursue educational opportunities in foreign countries (Sironi et al., 2019). The link between education and economic development and employability (SDG 1, SDG 8, SDG 16), inclusive education and lifelong learning (SDG 4), social inclusion and justice (SDG 16), eliminating discrimination and inequality (SDG 4, SDG 10), and worldwide collaboration (SDG 17) have also been contextualised in the Agenda 2030 (Kushnir & Nunes, 2022; Nicolai et al., 2017) through education primarily explored under SDG 4. This interconnected relationship among education, migration, and related matters concerning sustainable development necessitates governmental and intergovernmental organisations' dealing with the migration and education issues with a holistic approach that balances the interests and notices the challenges and opportunities (UNESCO, 2020). By unravelling the conceptual framework underpinning the scholarly sources in the context of global sustainable development and educational migration, this chapter strives to enhance the understanding of the intricate interplay of education, migration, and sustainable development and to provide a basis for informed decision-making and comprehensive strategies at governmental and intergovernmental levels.

6.3. Methodological Considerations

6.3.1. Research Design

This chapter aimed to describe the scholarly sources on migration in the field of education indexed in the WOS and published between 2015 and 2022, explore their collaboration trends, and reveal the conceptual structure of these studies in the context of international sustainable development. Therefore, a bibliometric methodology was employed to investigate the following research questions (RQs) as illustrated in Fig. 6.1:

RQ-1. What are the descriptive characteristics of the scholarly sources on migration in the area of education between 2015 and 2022?

RQ-2. What are the collaboration trends in the scholarly sources on migration in the area of education between 2015 and 2022?

RQ-3. How is the conceptual structure of the scholarly sources on migration in the area of education constituted between 2015 and 2022?

As depicted in Fig. 6.1, first, characteristics of migration studies in education between 2015 and 2022 were examined through descriptive analysis (*RQ-1*) and then the collaboration trends in these studies were investigated using citation, keywords, and co-authorship analyses (*RQ-2*). Based on the results of cluster analysis, the conceptual structure of migration studies was revealed (*RQ-3*).

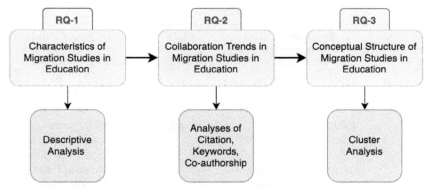

Fig. 6.1. Research Model. *Source*: Authors' own work.*

6.3.2. Identification of the Scholarly Sources

Based on the RQs within the scope of a bibliometric methodology, a strategy for the identification of the scholarly sources on migration in education was developed including the steps of selection of the database, keyword determination, formulation of the search string, specifications for inclusion and exclusion criteria, and finally the acquisition of the eligible studies to be included in the analyses to address RQs. Accordingly, in the first phase, the database was selected as the WOS because of its high-quality data providing software compatibility necessary for the bibliometric analyses. Second, keywords used in the database search were determined as 'migration' and 'education' with their possible equivalences. Then, the search string was formulated by employing the Boolean method. Subsequently, the inclusion and exclusion criteria were specified within the scope of the RQs as listed in Table 6.1.

Date range (Inc-1; Exc-1), WOS category (Inc-2; Exc-2), citation topics at the micro level (Inc-3; Exc-3), document type (Inc-4; Exc-4), publication language (Inc-5; Exc-5), and content compliance (Inc-6; Exc-6) were specified for the eligibility of the scholarly sources indexed in the WOS. The date range of the data was determined as the year 2015 when the SDGs were agreed upon at the COP21 Paris Climate Conference. The process of the implementation of the inclusion/exclusion criteria was organised by employing the Prisma flowchart as a guideline for reporting systematic reviews (Page et al., 2021) as illustrated in Fig. 6.2.

As presented in Fig. 6.2, the outcome of the determined keyword search with an appropriate search string resulted in 57,169 records indexed in the WOS database. As a result of processing the inclusion criteria, 55,219 documents

---

*See online for the color version of figures.

Table 6.1. Inclusion and Exclusion Criteria.

Code	Inclusion Criteria	Code	Exclusion Criteria
Inc-1	The date range was determined as 01.01.2015 and 31.12.2022.	Exc-1	Publication dates were outside the range of 01.01.2015 to 31.12.2022.
Inc-2	'Education/Educational Research' and 'Education Scientific Disciplines' were selected as the WOS categories for education.	Exc-2	Publications were categorised outside of 'Education/Educational Research' and 'Education Scientific Disciplines' in the WOS categories.
Inc-3	'6.11 Education & Educational Research' was selected for citation topics micro.	Exc-3	Citation topics micro did not fall under '6.11 Education & Educational Research'.
Inc-4	The document type was selected as 'articles'.	Exc-4	The publications which were not articles were excluded such as conference papers, etc.
Inc-5	Publication language was determined as English.	Exc-5	Publications were not written in the English language.
Inc-6	Publication context was checked if it was within the scope of RQs.	Exc-6	Publication context was falling outside the scope of the RQs.

Source: Authors' own work.

were eliminated for Exc-1, Exc-2, and Exc-3 in addition to the exclusion of 788 records for Exc-4 and Exc-5. Of 1,162 publications, 10 were not retrieved due to some missing components such as keywords or abstracts, and 161 were also eliminated for Exc-6 due to falling outside the scope of the RQs. Finally, 991 scholarly sources on migration were determined as the eligible data to be analysed in the field of education.

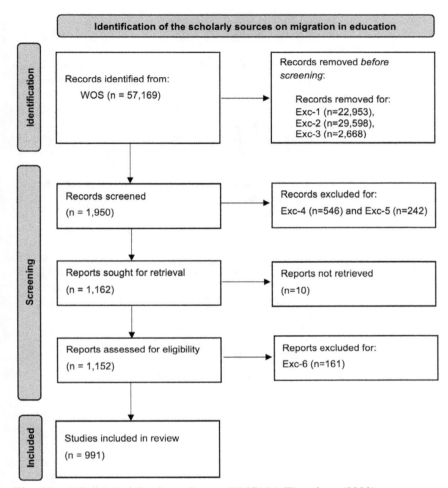

Fig. 6.2. Eligible Publications. *Source*: PRISMA Flowchart (2020).

6.3.3. Analysis of Identified Data Sources

A bibliometric methodology using VOSviewer for Windows v1.16 was implemented for the quantitative investigation of *RQ-1*, *RQ-2*, and *RQ-3*. Accordingly, to explore the characteristics of the identified data sources formulated as *RQ-1*, descriptive analyses were carried out to encapsulate and outline the principal features, patterns, and trends present within a dataset. The descriptive indicators, in the context of this study, included aspects such as the number of identified publications and citations per year, micro-level citation topics, the journals, and the number of authors contributing to the identified data sources.

Subsequently, it was aimed to scrutinise and interpret the patterns and dynamics of collaboration within the ambit of migration in educational research over a duration of seven years (2015–2022). By evaluating the trends in collaboration, the study sought to delineate patterns of cooperation and ascertain the nature of established collaborations for migration studies in education. To address *RQ-2*, network analysis was performed including analyses of citation, keyword usage, and country-wise co-authorship patterns. Thus, trends in citation networks and co-authorship focusing on 'the interactions among scholars in a research field' (Donthu et al., 2021) were examined by providing the visualisation of collaboration networks to pinpoint influential nodes and clusters within the research community.

Finally, to reveal the conceptual structure of migration studies in education, cluster analysis was carried out to address *RQ-3*. Cluster analysis, as an enrichment technique in bibliometric methodology, aims to create 'thematic or social groups' to classify objects or cases into relatively homogeneous groups, known as clusters, based on selected characteristics by using some techniques such as exploratory factor analysis (Donthu et al., 2021; Zupic & Čater, 2015). In other words, it is a family of algorithms designed to form groups such that the data points in the same group are more similar to each other than to those in other groups. Based on the results of the cluster analysis, the identified clusters including 'indicators that are mutually strongly correlated' were labelled, which is the process of naming each group with explanatory terms describing the common features in each cluster (Franceschet, 2009). Accordingly, the detected clusters were labelled within the scope of the related literature.

6.4. Results

6.4.1. Characteristics of Migration Studies in Education

Regarding the characteristics of migration studies in education, descriptive indicators such as distribution of publications and their citations, citation topics at the micro level, journals, and the number of authors contributing to these papers

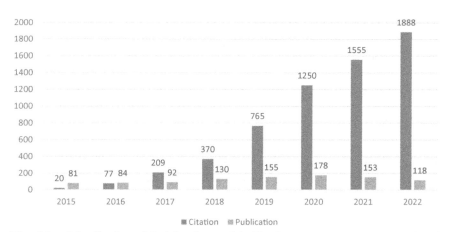

Fig. 6.3. Distribution of Publications With Citations per Year. *Source*: Authors' own work.

were analysed to address *RQ-1*. First, the distribution of the publications on migration in the field of education and the number of citations they received per year were examined as presented in Fig. 6.3.

As seen in Fig. 6.3, 991 articles were published on migration in the educational context in the WOS core collection between 2015 and 2022. The highest number of studies was conducted in 2020 ($n = 178$), and the highest number of citations for these articles on migration was received in 2022 ($n = 1,888$). An increasing trend has also been observed in the number of citations for the studies conducted on migration in the educational context since 2015. The escalating number of citations underscores the topical relevance of the subject matter and signifies a growing recognition within the academic community of the importance of understanding migration in education.

As provided by the WOS database, citation topics that are algorithmically derived citation clusters by the system were investigated for these 991 studies at the micro level. Accordingly, it was detected that the publications on migration in the educational field were divided into nine topics based on citation topics with micro-categorisation as listed in Table 6.2.

In Table 6.2, it was revealed that a variety of topics were indexed with a micro-categorisation approach for 991 articles on migration. Accordingly, the cited topic 'International Students' accounted for 272 articles with 27.45% of the total, ranked first on the list. 'Teacher Education' and 'School Leadership' contributed 170 articles (17.15%) and 164 articles (16.55%), respectively, to the overall sum. 'Intergenerational Mobility' represented 14.53% of the total with 144 articles. Additionally, the research topic featured a focus on 'Self-regulated Learning' ($n = 38$; 3.83%) and 'Science Education' ($n = 34$; 3.43%). The topics 'Critical

Table 6.2. Distribution of Micro-Level Citation Topics.

Citation Topics Micro	n	%
6.11.1255 International Students	272	27.45
6.11.190 Teacher Education	170	17.15
6.11.345 School Leadership	164	16.55
6.11.666 Intergenerational Mobility	144	14.53
6.11.31 Self-regulated Learning	38	3.83
6.11.295 Science Education	34	3.43
6.11.882 Critical Pedagogy	27	2.72
6.11.2357 Transformative Learning	23	2.32
6.11.2221 History Education	16	1.61
Total	**888**	**89.61**
Others	103	10.39
Grand total	**991**	**100.00**

Source: Authors' own work.

Table 6.3. Distribution of Migration Studies in Education By Journal[a].

Journal Title	n	%
Globalisation Societies and Education	32	3.23
Higher Education	31	3.13
Intercultural Education	28	2.83
Journal of International Students	21	2.12
Teaching and Teacher Education	21	2.12
Teachers College Record	19	1.92
Education Sciences	17	1.72
Discourse Studies in the Cultural Politics of Education	14	1.41
International Journal of Qualitative Studies in Education	14	1.41
International Review of Education	13	1.31
Compare: A Journal of Comparative and International Education	12	1.21
European Educational Research Journal	12	1.21
Frontiers in Education	12	1.21
International Journal of Educational Development	12	1.21
Multicultural Education Review	12	1.21
Studies in Higher Education	12	1.21
British Educational Research Journal	11	1.11
Theory and Research in Social Education	11	1.11
Educational Review	10	1.01
Journal of Studies in International Education	10	1.01
Total	**324**	**32.7**

[a]Journals with a share greater than 1% of the total. *Source*: Authors' own work.

Pedagogy', 'Transformative Learning', and 'History Education' made up the final three themes on the list, each contributing 2.72%, 2.32%, and 1.61%, respectively.

Journals having published 991 studies on migration in the field of education were identified as another descriptive indicator. The results of this analysis with a share greater than 1% of the total are presented in Table 6.3 with the number of published articles.

Table 6.3 lists the journals having published at least 10 migration studies with a share greater than 1% of the total publications ($n = 324$; 32.7%). Accordingly, the *Journal of Globalisation Societies and Education* received the highest rate with 32 articles, comprising 3.23%, followed closely by the *Journal of Higher Education* which produced 31 research papers (3.13%), accounting for the second-highest contribution. The third-placed journal, *Intercultural Education*, published 28 migration studies (2.83%). The journals *Teaching and Teacher Education* and *International Students* each produced 21 papers, accounting for 2.12% of the total publications.

Finally, the authors having conducted these 991 migration studies in education were examined according to the number of papers they contributed. It was detected that 991 migration studies were carried out by 1,961 authors, which means that most of the articles were written by different authors. Table 6.4 illustrates the diversity of authors according to the articles.

Table 6.4. Number of Authors Contributing to Papers.

Authors Contributing to …	n	%
8 articles	1	0.05
7 articles	1	0.05
6 articles	1	0.05
5 articles	3	0.15
4 articles	12	0.61
3 articles	36	1.84
2 articles	144	7.34
1 article	1,763	89.90
Total	**1,961**	**100.00**

Source: Authors' own work.

As observed in Table 6.4, 1,763 authors contributed to just one article (89.90%). In contrast, a far smaller set of authors contributed to multiple articles. For example, 144 authors, or 7.34%, of the total each wrote two articles. The proportion of authors conducting three research papers fell sharply to 36 (1.84%). By contributing to four articles, 12 authors (0.61%) made up the remaining. The number of authors contributing to more than four articles was quite limited. Three authors each took place in five publications, whereas only one author contributed to the remaining six, seven, and eight articles, representing just 0.05% of the entire publication.

6.4.2. Collaboration Trends in Migration Studies in Education

Scholarly collaborations enable researchers to benefit from one another's experience by exploring challenging RQs together and looking into chances for further research to optimise outputs. To comprehend the intellectual landscape and trends in academia, citation analysis is an essential tool for evaluating the significance and effect of a particular piece of research or author within a certain subject. In this respect, to address *RQ-2*, citation analysis, keyword usage, and co-authorship patterns across nations were accepted as the markers for the current research indicating collaboration trends. Therefore, citation analysis was

Table 6.5. Most-Cited Migration Studies in Education[a].

Authors	Title of Publication	TC	ACPY
Lörz et al. (2016)	Why do students from underprivileged families less often intend to study abroad?	92	11.50
Banks (2017)	Failed citizenship and transformative civic education	81	11.57
Jiani (2017)	Why and how international students choose Mainland China as a higher education study abroad destination	79	11.29
Hachfeld et al. (2015)	Should teachers be colour-blind? How multicultural and egalitarian beliefs differentially relate to aspects of teachers' professional competence for teaching in diverse classrooms	73	8.11
Morley et al. (2018)	Internationalisation and migrant academics: the hidden narratives of mobility	68	11.33
Jaquette and Curs (2015)	Creating the out-of-state university: Do public universities increase non-resident freshman enrolment in response to declining state appropriations?	66	7.33
Wen and Hu (2019)	The emergence of a regional education hub: Rationales of international students' choice of China as the study destination	65	13.00
Jerrim (2015)	An investigation of Western-born children of East Asian descent	57	6.33
Carlone et al. (2015)	Agency amidst formidable structures: How girls perform gender in science class	56	6.22
Yang Hansen and Gustafsson (2016)	Causes of educational segregation in Sweden–school choice or residential segregation	55	6.88
McNess et al. (2015)	Ethnographic dazzle' and the construction of the 'Other': revisiting dimensions of insider and outsider research for international and comparative education	54	6.00

(*Continued*)

Table 6.5. (*Continued*)

Authors	Title of Publication	TC	ACPY
Gay (2015)	The what, why, and how of culturally responsive teaching: International mandates, challenges, and opportunities	53	5.89
Umansky (2016)	An examination of the impact of classifying students as English learners	52	6.50
Lipura and Collins (2020)	Towards an integrative understanding of contemporary educational mobilities: A critical agenda for international student mobilities research	51	12.75
Stoessel et al. (2015)	Sociodemographic diversity and distance education: Who drops out from academic programs and why?	51	5.67
Yang (2018)	Compromise and complicity in international student mobility: The ethnographic case of Indian medical students at a Chinese university	50	8.33

[a]Papers with more than 50 citations.
Source: Authors' own work.

performed for 991 publications between 2015 and 2022, and the most influential papers on migration were detected in the field of education. Table 6.5 lists the publications with a total citation (TC) number of 50 or more with the average citation per year (ACPY).

According to Table 6.5, the article prepared by Lörz et al. (2016) received the highest number of citations (TC = 92; ACPY = 11.50), detected as the most-cited article. The research paper published by Banks (2017) was ranked second with 81 citations (ACPY = 11.57) followed by the article prepared by Jiani (2017) with 79 citations (ACPY = 11.29).

Totally, 16 scholarly sources were identified as the most influential migration research in education, and a keyword analysis of 991 scholarly publications was performed, which offers an organised and data-driven perception of the content, trends, and research gaps within the field of study. The most common top 10 keywords used in the 991 scholarly works on migration are listed in Table 6.6.

As indicated in Table 6.6, the most frequently occurring keyword was 'Migration' appearing in 61 instances. 'Higher Education' was used 58 times listed in the second order. 'International students' appeared 43 times, while the keyword 'Refugees' was used 34 times, indicating a focus on contemporary social issues. The terms 'Immigration' and 'Diversity' were stated 27 and 26 times, respectively, shedding light on intercultural aspects of education. There were 25 occurrences of

Table 6.6. Results of Keyword Examination.

Keywords	Occurrences
Migration	61
Higher education	58
International students	43
Refugees	34
Immigration	27
Diversity	26
Education	25
International students	24
Equity	20
Social justice	20
Total	**338**
Others	2,446
Grand total	**2,784**

Source: Authors' own work.

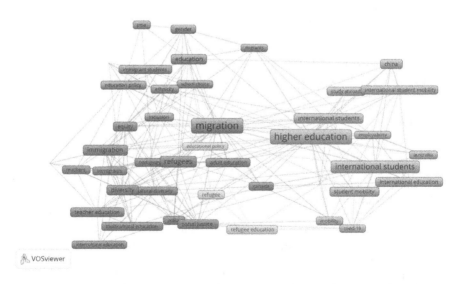

Note: The colours represent clusters, the lines represent connections, the size of the circles and labels represents the weight/importance of the articles, and the distances between them represent the closeness/distance of the relationship between two articles.

Fig. 6.4. Mapping Results of Keywords. *Source*: Authors' own work, using VOSviewer software.

the term 'education' alone. Finally, the 20 appearances of the keywords 'Equity' and 'Social Justice', respectively, highlighted the social emphasis in several publications. All these stated keywords amounted to 338 in number overall. Additionally, there were 2,446 occurrences of other keywords not listed in Table 6.6, making up a significant portion of the total of 2,784 keywords.

The examination of keywords of the articles on migration in the field of education additionally revealed a variety of important themes. In Fig. 6.4, it can be observed that these keywords are grouped into four different clusters, indicating their interconnectedness.

Fig. 6.4 illustrates an improved understanding of the links, connections, and significance among articles on migration. Accordingly, the green cluster seemed to focus on international student mobility, especially between China and Australia. The themes appeared to revolve around the mobility of students for higher education, especially international students, and the various factors that affected it, such as 'study abroad' programmes and 'employability'. The inclusion of 'Covid-19' suggested that the cluster might also touch upon the impact of the pandemic on student mobility and international education. The blue cluster appeared to be centred on the intersection of education and migration. It brought up topics related to education policy, school choice, and the educational experiences of migrants and ethnic minorities. The keyword 'PISA' (Programme for International Student Assessment) could imply a focus on standardised testing and how various demographics performed, potentially related to migrants or different ethnic groups. The cluster in red leaned towards themes of social justice in education, incorporating the elements like 'equity', 'immigration', 'refugees', and 'adult education'. There was also a strong focus on pedagogical approaches to cultural diversity, inclusion, and multicultural education. The yellow cluster appeared to be narrowly focused on the subject of 'refugee education' and educational policies surrounding it. Due to its smaller size, it might indicate either a niche area of focus or an emerging field that has not been as extensively covered as the other topics. In general, Australia, China, and Canada were explicitly mentioned, suggesting that the studies might have a geographical focus. Several themes like 'migration', 'policy', and 'education' appeared across the clusters indicating the interconnectedness of these issues.

Finally, co-authorship analysis was conducted to explore the country variable; accordingly, the number of articles published by country with the total and average citations of these articles were examined and the countries with more than 20 migration studies in education are presented in Table 6.7.

The distribution of co-authorship across different countries revealed the collaboration trends in migration research in the field of education between 2015 and 2022. The USA stood out with the highest number of documents at 304, garnering 2,095 citations and averaging about 6.89 citations per document. England, with 100 articles and 1,120 citations, held the second on the list but showed the highest mean citations of 11.20 per document. These two countries suggested a significant global impact of research on migration in the field of education. Australia closely followed England with 99 articles, accumulating 861 citations with a mean citation count of 8.70. Canada contributed 89 publications with 457

Table 6.7. Results of Co-authorship Analysis By Country.

Country[a]	Continent	Articles	Citations	Mean Citations
USA	North America	304	2,095	6.89
England	Europe	100	1,120	11.20
Australia	Australia	99	861	8.70
Canada	North America	89	457	5.13
Germany	Europe	49	470	9.59
China	Asia	45	469	10.42
Spain	Europe	45	280	6.22
Sweden	Europe	39	295	7.56
Norway	Europe	33	273	8.27
Netherlands	Europe	27	204	7.56
Finland	Europe	25	90	3.60
Turkey	Asia	24	132	5.50
Israel	Asia	22	180	8.18

[a]Countries with more than 20 articles.
Source: Authors' own work.

citation numbers averaging 5.13 per paper. Germany's 49 and China's 45 articles had notably higher mean citations, 9.59 and 10.42, respectively, which displayed the impact of their research contributions. Spain and Sweden each conducted 45 and 39 migration research articles, respectively, with an average of 6.22 and 7.56 citations per document. Norway and the Netherlands had relatively high mean citations, 8.27 and 7.56, respectively. Finally, Finland, Turkey, and Israel had fewer articles and average citation numbers, yet contributed meaningfully to the corpus of research. In Fig. 6.5, the visualisation of these collaborative relationships between countries is depicted by mapping on VOSviewer.

As mapped in Fig. 6.5, the countries in the green cluster were all located in the Asia-Pacific region. Malaysia, Singapore, Thailand, and Australia are geographically close with strong economic and academic ties, which suggests a strong regional collaboration in research. The purple cluster included English-speaking countries such as New Zealand, Canada, and England with strong historical, cultural, and linguistic ties. This might indicate a preference or ease of collaboration between countries with a shared language and similar academic and research cultures. China, South Korea, and the United States, in the blue cluster, were major players in global research with strong economic ties. The cluster in dark blue included Western European countries such as Finland, Germany, Switzerland, Belgium, and the Netherlands known for their strong academic and research institutions. These countries have had a history of collaboration and similar socio-political contexts, which might facilitate research collaboration. The countries in the orange, yellow, and red clusters had different languages and political

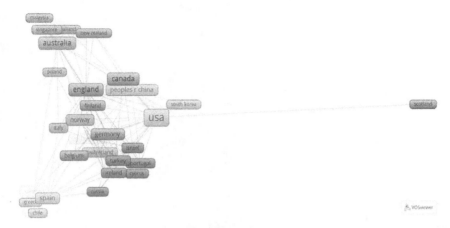

Note: The colours represent clusters, the lines represent connections, the size of the circles and labels represents the weight/importance of the articles, and the distances between them represent the closeness/distance of the relationship between two articles.

Fig. 6.5. Collaborative Relationships Across Countries. *Source*: Authors' own work, using VOSviewer software.

contexts; therefore, it can be claimed that the collaboration might be based on specific research areas or international projects. The clusters illustrated in Fig. 6.5 indicated that international research collaboration was influenced by a number of factors including geographical proximity, linguistic and cultural ties, shared research interests, and participation in international projects.

6.4.3. Conceptual Structure of Migration Studies in Education

To address *RQ-3* for the identification of the conceptual structure of migration studies in education, it was determined that there were 222 articles that received at least 10 citations based on the results illustrated in Fig. 6.5. In this context, cluster analysis was carried out on VOSviewer, and it was detected that 25 publications were found interrelated among these 222 articles. The connection map of these 25 interrelated articles is presented in Fig. 6.6.

After a visual examination of the articles identified as interconnected in Fig. 6.6, it was determined that they were grouped into a total of seven different clusters. The red cluster centred around the studies conducted by Mulvey (2021), Sidhu and Ishikawa (2022), Waters (2018), and Yang (2020). The cluster in green was composed of the research by Gunter and Raghuram (2018), Jöns (2018), King and Sondhi (2018), and Page and Chahboun (2019). The four studies carried out by Chankseliani (2018a, 2018b), Lee and Sehoole (2015), and Lee (2017) were interconnected in the cluster illustrated in dark blue. The yellow cluster consisted of the studies by Chen (2016), Lipura and Collins (2020), Ortiga (2018), and Yang (2018). The cluster in purple revealed a connection among the research conducted by Jokila (2015), Xu and Montgomery (2019), Yu and Zhang (2016), and Yu et al. (2021). The three publications were accumulated in the blue cluster

Note: The colours represent clusters, the lines represent connections, the size of the circles and labels represents the weight/importance of the articles, and the distances between them represent the closeness/distance of the relationship between two articles.

Fig. 6.6. Connection Map of Interrelated Migration Studies in Education.
Source: Authors' own work, using VOSviewer software.

(Lee, 2019; Ma & Pan, 2015; Yang, 2022). The last cluster included two studies highlighted in orange (Jiani, 2017; Wen & Hu, 2019). After a rigorous examination of all these clusters with their connected articles, representative labels were assigned to each cluster as shown in Fig. 6.7.

Fig. 6.7 presents the results of the cluster analysis, revealing distinct themes and research focuses within the realm of migration in educational research. Each cluster was defined by a set of keywords capturing the central themes and concepts addressed in the articles grouped within that cluster (C). Accordingly, 'Discourse and Politics of International Student Mobility' (C1) explored the complexities of global student mobility, particularly in the context of China and Africa. 'Trans/national Academic Mobilities and International Study' (C2) centred on the mobility of academics and students across national boundaries. 'Regional Dynamics and Neo-Nationalism in Educational Mobility' (C3) focused on the regional and geopolitical influences on student mobility. 'Factors Shaping International Student Mobility' (C4) investigated the multifaceted factors influencing student mobility decisions. 'Cultural Adaptation and Internationalisation in Higher Education' (C5) probed the intersection of culture, globalisation, and internationalisation in higher education. 'Capital Accumulation in Education Mobility' (C6) revolved around the accumulation of global linguistic and cultural capital within educational migration. 'Motivational Factors for International Students' (C7)

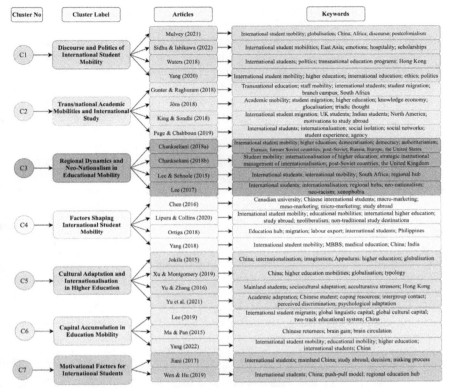

Fig. 6.7. Results of Cluster Analysis. *Source*: Authors' own work.

examined the decision-making processes of international students, exploring factors that influence their choice of study destination.

6.5. Discussion

Due to the dynamic relationship between migration and education, it is important to investigate how education can both address the problems caused by migration and maximise its potential for sustainable development. Thus, this chapter explored the characteristics, collaboration trends, and conceptual structure of migration studies in education from 2015 to 2022 within the scope of international sustainable development. First, 991 articles were identified within this period, and a notable increase was detected in both the number of publications and citations over time. The rise in citations received by these articles over the years signifies the increasing relevance of migration in education. This trend underlines the recognition of migration's impact on education systems, and it necessitates in-depth research to address related challenges. The micro-level analysis of citation topics revealed the prominence of 'International Students' as the most-cited topic, followed by 'Teacher Education' and 'School Leadership', which indicates the significance of these areas in migration studies within the educational context, and the multifaceted aspects of migration's influence on education. The study also provided insights into the distribution of publications across journals, which contributed to the dissemination of research on migration in education and the promotion of their visibility. Additionally, the diversity of authors contributing to these studies was also highlighted, with a majority of authors contributing to only one article, which underscores the diversity of voices and perspectives in this field by demonstrating the collaborative and multidisciplinary nature of migration studies in education.

Second, collaboration trends in the collected scholarly sources were investigated through citation analysis, co-authorship patterns, and international collaborations. The most influential papers on migration in education were identified through citation analysis. The top-cited articles cover a wide range of topics, including student intentions to study abroad, civic education, international student choice, multicultural competence among teachers, and the narratives of migrant academics (e.g., Jöns, 2018; Mulvey, 2021; Wen & Hu, 2019). Keyword analysis revealed the prominent themes and areas of focus within migration studies. The prevalence of keywords like 'Migration', 'Higher Education', and 'International Students' underscores their centrality in the research discourse. Additionally, keywords such as 'Refugees', 'Diversity', 'Equity', and 'Social Justice' reflect the field's commitment to addressing contemporary social issues and fostering inclusivity in education (Lipura & Collins, 2020; Yang, 2020). The United States, England, and Australia were found as prominent contributors, which demonstrates the global reach of migration research in education. The collaboration clusters revealed regional and thematic patterns influenced by factors such as geographic proximity, shared language, and research interests.

Finally, the study identified the conceptual structure of migration studies in education through cluster analysis. Seven distinct clusters emerged, each representing a specific research focus within the field. These clusters encompassed topics such as international student mobility, transnational academic mobilities, regional dynamics, factors shaping student mobility, cultural adaptation in higher education, capital accumulation in education mobility, and motivational factors for international students. These clusters offered a comprehensive view of the diverse research landscape within migration studies in education for sustainable development. The main focus of sustainable development is to balance the requirements of today's people without sacrificing the capacity of the next generations to meet their own needs (WCED, 1987). In parallel with this fundamental statement, these clusters are closely related to the SDGs such as many students migrating to act as a driving force for quality education (Mosler Vidal & Laczko, 2022), cultural understanding and exchange (Abdulkadyrov et al., 2021), human capital development and capacity-building effect (Jöns, 2018; Olowookere et al., 2022; Payab et al., 2023).

6.5.1. Discourse and Politics of International Student Mobility

International student mobility plays a critical role in the development of human capital. As students from diverse backgrounds gain access to higher education institutions (HEIs) worldwide, they acquire knowledge and skills that are essential for sustainable development (Mbithi et al., 2021). This cluster revolved around the discourse and political dimensions of international student mobility (Mulvey, 2021; Sidhu & Ishikawa, 2022; Waters, 2018; Yang, 2020). The articles within this cluster delved into the complex interplay between globalisation, international student mobility, and political dynamics by exploring how discourses surrounding migration impact students' experiences and how postcolonial perspectives influence educational mobility. For instance, Mulvey (2021) examined the politics of international student mobility, while Sidhu and Ishikawa (2022) investigated emotions and hospitality in East Asian international student mobilities. Waters (2018) addressed politics in transnational education programmes, particularly in the context of Hong Kong, and Yang (2020) discussed the ethical and political considerations in international student mobility.

The human capital model (Becker, 1964) posits that education is an investment individuals make to maximise their lifetime earnings. In the context of international student mobility, this model suggests that students migrate to cultivate skills or credentials that may not be readily available in their home country, and this is, therefore, crucial for the development of human capital and the achievement of SDGs (Payab et al., 2023). Human capital development is a key strategy in the global effort of eradicating severe poverty and fostering more inclusive communities (World Bank, 2023). It provides students with opportunities to gain global competence and prepares them for culturally diverse working environments (Abdulkadyrov et al., 2021). Through international mobility experiences, students can enhance their global competence and contribute to the sustainable development of their countries (Olowookere et al., 2022). However, there are challenges and barriers to international student mobility that need to be addressed (Kjellgren & Richter, 2022). By redesigning international student mobility programmes and providing adequate support, HEIs can better support the development of global competence among students (Ugnich et al., 2021). Therefore, international student mobility should be considered a valuable tool for both human capital development and the achievement of SGDs.

6.5.2. Trans/national Academic Mobilities and International Study

Transnational academic mobilities and international studies refer to educational and academic activities that include people, organisations, and knowledge that travel within or across national boundaries (Angouri, 2023), which is the focus of this cluster (Gunter & Raghuram, 2018; Jöns, 2018; King & Sondhi, 2018; Page & Chahboun, 2019). The articles explored the intricate dynamics of staff mobility, branch campuses, and student migration by investigating how globalisation impacts academic mobility and discussing the role of higher education in the global knowledge economy. Gunter and Raghuram (2018) investigated transnational education and staff mobility, while Jöns (2018) examined academic mobility and the knowledge economy. King and Sondhi (2018) explored motivations for international student migration, whereas Page and Chahboun (2019) highlighted social networks and student experiences in the context of internationalisation.

Transnational academic mobilities and international studies contribute to several concerns regarding sustainability, such as facilitating knowledge transfer, capacity-building, collaborations in research, and global citizenship understanding (Angouri, 2023; Sutrisno & Pillay, 2015). They promote intercultural considerations in research and teaching (Jones et al., 2016), give a chance to integrate global and local concerns in research and teaching, and enhance research and educational initiatives for sustainability (Caniglia et al., 2017). Accordingly, these characteristics allow transnational academic mobilities and international studies useful instruments in the effort to create a more sustainable and just world.

6.5.3. Regional Dynamics and Neo-Nationalism in Educational Mobility

Neo-racism, the discrimination against international students, and neo-nationalism or new nationalism, the 'national order in the new global economy' (Lee, 2017), regional dynamics representing background features related to home countries or regions have significant and concerning effects on international higher education, global integration, and sustainable development (Douglass, 2021; Lee, 2017). In this context, this cluster examined regional dynamics and neo-nationalism's influence on educational mobility (Chankseliani, 2018a, 2018b; Lee, 2017; Lee & Sehoole, 2015). The articles explored international student mobility within the context of former Soviet countries, Eurasia, and South Africa by discussing the relationship between internationalisation, regional hubs, and the rise of neo-nationalism and neo-racism. Chankseliani (2018a) addressed international student mobility and democratisation in former Soviet countries, while Chankseliani (2018b) focused on strategic institutional management of internationalisation. Lee and Sehoole (2015) examined international mobility in South Africa, and Lee (2017) discussed regional hubs, neo-nationalism, and xenophobia.

Numerous difficulties may be encountered by an international student who is adjusting to a new setting, either because of the student himself/herself or the surroundings. Many foreign students encounter xenophobic actions and negative stereotyping, as well as a sense of insecurity (Gopal, 2016; Koo et al., 2023). Regional dynamics can also influence how well international students manage while studying abroad (Ramia, 2021). It is essential to remain conscious that while some nations may find an approach to reconcile national interests with international cooperation and the SDGs, neo-nationalism would have a detrimental effect on sustainable development in light of the values of equity, inclusivity, and global partnership. Therefore, it is essential to address regional dynamics and neo-nationalism carefully and thoroughly in the context of educational mobility.

6.5.4. Factors Shaping International Student Mobility

A range of multifaceted dynamics, including social, cultural, organisational, and individual reasons, affects the mobility of international students (OECD, 2015; Perez-Encinas et al., 2021). Consistently, this cluster explored the factors that shape international student mobility (Chen, 2016; Lipura & Collins,

2020; Ortiga, 2018; Yang, 2018). The articles within this cluster explored various aspects of student mobility, including marketing strategies, non-traditional study destinations, and the impact of migration and labour export on education hubs. Chen (2016) focused on marketing strategies and study abroad, while Lipura and Collins (2020) discussed educational mobilities and non-traditional study destinations. Ortiga (2018) examined education hubs and migration in the Philippines, whereas Yang (2018) explored medical education and international student mobility.

Economic opportunities in the host country (Souto-Otero et al., 2013), familiarity with the culture and social support networks, quality of the host university and the city, and the work and career opportunities (Perez-Encinas et al., 2021), the impact of natural regulations (Angouri, 2023) could be listed as the most common contextual factors for international student mobility. Policymakers and educational institutions may develop policies and programmes that support the SDGs by taking these factors into account in the context of international student mobility. These initiatives can encourage fair access to high-quality education, lessen inequities, increase international collaboration, and improve the well-being of both local populations and overseas students.

6.5.5. Cultural Adaptation and Internationalisation in Higher Education

Cultural adaptation in the realm of international student mobility often entails foreign students and scholars adapting to the culture and educational atmosphere of the host nation or institution (Martini, 2021; Smith & Khawaja, 2011). Similarly, this cluster centred on cultural adaptation and internationalisation in HEIs (Jokila, 2015; Xu & Montgomery, 2019; Yu & Zhang, 2016; Yu et al., 2021). The articles investigated the role of internationalisation in higher education and how students adapted to new cultural environments by discussing concepts like global imagination, typologies of higher education mobilities, and sociocultural adaptation. Jokila (2015) examined the internationalisation of higher education using Appadurai's ideas, while Xu and Montgomery (2019) discussed mobilities in higher education and globalisation. Yu and Zhang (2016) delved into sociocultural adaptation of mainland students in Hong Kong, while Yu et al. (2021) explored academic and psychological adaptation among Chinese students.

To improve the acculturation of international students, it is crucial to focus on group and individual characteristics, stressors, coping mechanisms, and social support (Smith & Khawaja, 2011). Consistently, the realisation of the potential of international students' acculturation can act as a catalyst for cross-cultural awareness, global citizenship, and sustainable development as it could foster empathy, cross-cultural communication, and a more expansive worldview.

6.5.6. Capital Accumulation in Education Mobility

Capital accumulation in the context of international educational mobility refers to the process by which people, institutions, and nations accumulate and build a variety of capital (e.g., human, social, cultural, and economic capital) (Goodwin, 2003), through their participation in international educational opportunities. Accordingly, this cluster focused on capital accumulation within the context of educational mobility (Lee, 2019; Ma & Pan, 2015; Yang, 2022). The articles highlighted the global linguistic and cultural capital's role in shaping international student mobility, particularly within China's two-track educational system. The discussions extended to brain gain, brain circulation, and the accumulation of human capital through educational mobility. Lee (2019) discussed global linguistic and cultural capital among international student migrants, while Ma and Pan (2015) examined brain gain and brain circulation. Yang (2022) addressed capital accumulation and international student mobility in China.

The accumulation of crucial capital, such as gaining knowledge, credentials, and skills, that can contribute to employability; the development of social capital by creating international networks and relationships; and the expansion of educational opportunities and research collaborations are all part of the process of international student mobility that go beyond simply achieving a credit or degree (Bamberger, 2019; Goodwin, 2003; Sidhu et al., 2015). The idea of human capital development is about prospective societal benefits as well as enhanced personal advantages like income for graduates (McMahon, 2009). Therefore, capital accumulation through international mobility supports sustainable development by cultivating economic growth, reducing poverty, improving education, fostering knowledge transfer, and international collaboration.

6.5.7. Motivational Factors for International Students

The push–pull theory of international students by McMahon (1992) and the rational choice theory by Eriksson (2011) are frequently employed theories that explain individual factors of international students' choice to pursue education overseas. Consistently, this cluster also deepens the understanding centred on the motivational factors influencing international students' decisions to study abroad (Jiani, 2017; Wen & Hu, 2019). The articles within this cluster investigated students' decision-making processes by exploring push–pull models and the emergence of regional education hubs. The decision-making dynamics and the factors that attracted international students to specific study destinations were discussed extensively. Jiani (2017) examined motivational factors among mainland Chinese students studying abroad, while Wen and Hu (2019) discussed the push–pull model and regional education hubs in China.

The motivational dynamics of studying abroad are much more complicated than anticipated, and they need to be considered in a wider psychological and social framework (Yue & Lu, 2022). Understanding the motivations of international students and the variables influencing their choice of regional hubs could enable educational institutions, governments, and organisations to focus their efforts on the objectives of this varied group of students. This orchestration may result in more focused endeavours, partnerships, and projects that support sustainable development at the local, regional, and international levels.

6.6. Concluding Remarks

Increasing rates of international migration create complex issues in education as an ongoing crisis that calls for comprehensive social, political, and economic approaches. Equitable access to education, language obstacles, and the creation of inclusive settings are primary challenges that educational institutions face. From an economic perspective, nations need to plan to minimise any risks while maximising the advantages of migrant labour. The intricate interactions among these elements highlight the need for an all-encompassing strategy that goes beyond conventional educational frameworks and addresses the wider socio-economic ramifications of global migration. In this chapter, the objective was to outline the overarching patterns of relevant scholarly sources within the realm of education and migration, as indexed in the WOS between 2015 and 2022. It sought to investigate the trends in collaboration among these sources and delve into the conceptual framework underpinning these studies within the context of international sustainable development. To accomplish this, a bibliometric methodology was employed for an in-depth exploration and analysis of these publications; 991 studies on migration within the realm of education were descriptively analysed by examining various aspects such as the distribution of publications alongside their respective citations, the specific citation topics at a micro level, the journals disseminating these works, and the extent of authorship involvement in these publications.

In addition, a citation analysis was conducted to unveil the prevailing collaboration trends within the current research landscape and pinpoint the most influential papers in the field of education-related migration. Lastly, cluster analysis was employed using VOSviewer, revealing the interconnectedness of 25 publications that collectively comprised seven distinct clusters, each of which was discussed and approached as significant arguments for international sustainable development. This chapter underscores the valuable contribution of these publications to the broader realm of global sustainable development, providing a more comprehensive understanding of the multifaceted relationship between migration and education.

6.7. Implications and Future Directions

The sources investigated in this study shed light on the comprehension of migration in the educational context by endeavouring to articulate the interplay with sustainable development. The results suggest a few approaches for further research regarding strategy and methodology. The research area of migration and education has been dominated by the studies conducted for HEIs. It is clearly observed that higher education plays a central role in migration and education research in terms of study numbers, research trends, and the interaction of the studies. While this key role of HEIs is crucial for the sustainability of development, it also demonstrates that HEIs are stakeholders that must be included in the planning, implementation, and evaluation attempts for sustainable development by national and international policymakers and authorities.

Moreover, it is also worthy of attention in the limited impactful research conducted in other education levels, which may be indicated as a barrier to internationally sustain development.

Additionally, the findings in this chapter revealed that the geographic distribution of the scholarly sources is also limited, which could be due to the density of Western-dominant studies and journals in this field. However, it is also notable that the host countries conducted, respectively, more research than the home countries, which demonstrates a research gap for the educational impacts of migration and loss of human capital in the countries of origin.

Finally, there are some limitations of this study resulting from its methodology. This bibliometric review study concentrated on the scholarly research related to migration in the field of education indexed in the WOS between 2015 and 2022. Consequently, the findings are limited only to these sources. The study is also limited to peer-reviewed articles published in English. Future research in other databases with a wider time range could enlarge their scope and include publications in various languages to expand the existing knowledge base.

References

Abdulkadyrov, A. S., Eremina, I. Y., & Chuprova, A. V. (2021). Human capital management as a basis for global mobility for sustainable economic development. In J. V Ragulina, A. A. Khachaturyan, A. S. Abdulkadyrov, & Z. S. Babaeva (Eds.), *Sustainable development of modern digital economy: Perspectives from Russian experiences* (pp. 179–188). Springer International Publishing. https://doi.org/10.1007/978-3-030-70194-9_18

Angouri, J. (2023). *Transnational collaboration and mobility in higher education: Looking back–looking forward.* The Guild Insight Paper No. 4. The Guild of European Research Intensive Universities and Bern Open Publishing. http://dx.doi.org/10.48350/183223

Arjona-Pelado, I., & Atnashev, V. (2021). Challenges of migration into the European Union and proposal of solution through education. In R. Bolgov, V. Atnashev, Y. Gladkiy, A. Leete, A. Tsyb, & S. Pogodin (Eds.), *Proceedings of topical issues in international political geography* (pp. 13–22). Springer International Publishing. ISBN 978-3-030-78690-8.

Arnot, M., Schneider, C., & Welply, O. (2023). *Introduction – Education, mobilities and migration: People, ideas and resources.* Retrieved August 19, 2023, from https://aru.figshare.com/articles/chapter/Introduction._Education_mobilities_and_migration_people_ideas_and_resources/23757627.

Bamberger, A. (2019). Accumulating cosmopolitan and ethnic identity capital through international student mobility. *Studies in Higher Education, 45*(7), 1–13. https://doi.org/10.1080/03075079.2019a.1597037.

Banks, J. A. (2017). Failed citizenship and transformative civic education. *Educational Researcher, 46*(7), 366–377. https://doi.org/10.3102/0013189X17726741.

Becker, G. S. (1964). *Human capital: A theoretical and empirical analysis, with special reference to education.* University of Chicago Press.

Benson, A. (2019). Migrant teachers and classroom encounters: Processes of intercultural learning. *London Review of Education, 17*(1), 1–13. https://doi.org/10.18546/LRE.17.1.01

Bernard, A., & Bell, M. (2018). *Internal migration and education: A cross-national comparison*. ArXiv: General Economics. https://api.semanticscholar.org/CorpusID:85529861

Bilecen, B. (2020). Education and migration. In T. Bastia & R. Skeldon (Eds.), *Routledge handbook of migration and development* (pp. 242–250). Routledge. https://doi.org/10.4324/9781315276908-22

Caniglia, G., Luederitz, C., Groß, M., Muhr, M., John, B., Keeler, L. W., von Wehrden, H., Laubichler, M., Wiek, A., & Lang, D. (2017). Transnational collaboration for sustainability in higher education: Lessons from a systematic review. *Journal of Cleaner Production, 168*, 764–779. https://doi.org/10.1016/j.jclepro.2017.07.256

Carlone, H. B., Johnson, A., & Scott, C. M. (2015). Agency amidst formidable structures: How girls perform gender in science class. *Journal of Research in Science Teaching, 52*(4), 474–488. https://doi.org/10.1002/tea.21224

Chamakalayil, L., & Riegel, C. (2016). Negotiating potentials and limitations in education in transnational migration contexts: A case study. *European Education, 48*(2), 120–136. https://doi.org/10.1080/10564934.2016.1200933

Chankseliani, M. (2018a). The politics of student mobility: Links between outbound student flows and the democratic development of post-Soviet Eurasia. *International Journal of Educational Development, 62*, 281–288. https://doi.org/10.1016/j.ijedudev.2018.07.006

Chankseliani, M. (2018b). Four rationales of HE internationalization: Perspectives of UK universities on attracting students from former Soviet countries. *Journal of Studies in International Education, 22*(1), 53–70. https://doi.org/10.1177/1028315317725806

Chen, J. M. (2016). Three levels of push-pull dynamics among Chinese international students' decision to study abroad in the Canadian context. *Journal of International Students, 7*(1), 113–135. https://doi.org/10.32674/jis.v7i1.248

Donthu, N., Kumar, S., Mukherjee, D., Pandey, N., & Lim, W. M. (2021). How to conduct a bibliometric analysis: An overview and guidelines. *Journal of Business Research, 133*, 285–296. https://doi.org/10.1016/j.jbusres.2021.04.070

Douglass, J. A. (2021). *Neo-nationalism and universities: Populists, autocrats, and the future of higher education*. Johns Hopkins University Press.

du Plooy, D. R., Lyons, A., & Kashima, E. S. (2020). Social capital and the well-being of migrants to Australia: Exploring the role of generalised trust and social network resources. *International Journal of Intercultural Relations, 79*, 1–12. https://doi.org/10.1016/j.ijintrel.2020.07.001

Dustmann, C., & Glitz, A. (2011). Chapter 4 – Migration and education. In E. A. Hanushek, S. Machin, & L. Woessmann (Eds.), *Handbook of the economics of education* (pp. 327–439). Elsevier. https://doi.org/10.1016/B978-0-444-53444-6.00004-3

English, L. M., & Mayo, P. (Eds.). (2021). LLL challenges: Responding to migration and the sustainable development goals. In *Lifelong learning, global social justice, and sustainability* (pp. 93–116). Springer International Publishing. https://doi.org/10.1007/978-3-030-65778-9_7

Eriksson, L. (2011). *Rational choice theory: Potential and limits*. Palgrave Macmillan.

Franceschet, M. (2009). A cluster analysis of scholar and journal bibliometric indicators. *Journal of the American Society for Information Science and Technology, 60*(10), 1950–1964. https://doi.org/10.1002/asi.21152

Gay, G. (2015). The what, why, and how of culturally responsive teaching: International mandates, challenges, and opportunities. *Multicultural Education Review, 7*(3), 123–139. https://doi.org/10.1080/2005615X.2015.1072079

Gomellini, M., & Ó Gráda, C. (2019). Brain drain and brain gain in Italy and Ireland in the age of mass migration. In D. Mitch & G. Cappelli (Eds.), *Globalization and the rise of mass education* (pp. 163–191). Springer International Publishing. https://doi.org/10.1007/978-3-030-25417-9_6

Goodwin, N. R. (2003). *Five kinds of capital: Useful concepts for sustainable development.* Working Paper No. 03-07. Retrieved August 20, 2023, from https://ageconsearch.umn.edu/record/15595?ln=en

Gopal, A. (2016). Academic experiences of international graduate students: The Canadian perspective in the context of internationalization. In K. Bista & C. Foster (Eds.), *Exploring the social and academic experiences of international students in higher education institutions* (pp. 21–37). IGI Global. https://doi.org/10.4018/978-1-4666-9749-2.ch002

Gunter, A., & Raghuram, P. (2018). International study in the global south: Linking institutional, staff, student, and knowledge mobilities. *Globalisation, Societies and Education, 16*(2), 192–207. https://doi.org/10.1080/14767724.2017.1401453

Hachfeld, A., Hahn, A., Schroeder, S., Anders, Y., & Kunter, M. (2015). Should teachers be colorblind? How multicultural and egalitarian beliefs differentially relate to aspects of teachers' professional competence for teaching in diverse classrooms. *Teaching and Teacher Education, 48,* 44–55. https://doi.org/10.1016/j.tate.2015.02.001

Hatton, T. J., & Williamson, J. G. (1998). *The age of mass migration: Causes and economic impact.* Oxford University Press. ISBN 0-19-511651-8.

International Organization for Migration (IOM). (2022). *World migration report 2022.* Retrieved September 3, 2023, from https://worldmigrationreport.iom.int/wmr-2022-interactive/

International Organization for Migration (IOM). (2023, September 4). *About migration.* https://www.iom.int/about-migration

Jacobs, E. (2022). The homogenizing and diversifying effects of migration policy in the internationalization of higher education. *Higher Education, 83*(2), 339–355. https://doi.org/10.1007/s10734-020-00658-4

Jaquette, O., & Curs, B. R. (2015). Creating the out-of-state university: Do public universities increase nonresident freshman enrollment in response to declining state appropriations? *Research in Higher Education, 56,* 535–565. http://www.jstor.org/stable/24572033

Jerrim, J. (2015). Why do East Asian children perform so well in PISA? An investigation of Western-born children of East Asian descent. *Oxford Review of Education, 41*(3), 310–333. https://doi.org/10.1080/03054985.2015.1028525

Jiani, M. A. (2017). Why and how international students choose Mainland China as a higher education study abroad destination. *Higher Education, 74,* 563–579. https://doi.org/10.1007/s10734-016-0066-0

Jokila, S. (2015). The internationalization of higher education with Chinese characteristics: Appadurai's ideas explored. *Asia Pacific Journal of Education, 35*(1), 125–139. https://doi.org/10.1080/02188791.2014.940029

Jones, B., Power, A., Gray, T., Downey, G., Hall, T., & Truong, S. (2016). If you build it, they may not come: Why Australian university students do not take part in outbound mobility experiences. *Journal of University Teaching and Learning Practice, 13*(3). https://doi.org/10.53761/1.13.3.9

Jöns, H. (2018). Boundary-crossing academic mobilities in glocal knowledge economies: New research agendas based on triadic thought. *Globalisation, Societies and Education, 16*(2), 151–161. https://doi.org/10.1080/14767724.2017.1413977

King, R., & Sondhi, G. (2018). International student migration: A comparison of UK and Indian students' motivations for studying abroad. *Globalisation, Societies and Education, 16*(2), 176–191. https://doi.org/10.1080/14767724.2017.1405244.

Kjellgren, B., & Richter, T. (2022). Redesigning international student mobility for global competence development. In *2022 IEEE global engineering education conference (EDUCON)* (pp. 1104–1112). https://doi.org/10.1109/EDUCON52537.2022.9766799

Koo, K. K., Yao, C. W., & Gong, H. J. (2023). 'It is not my fault': Exploring experiences and perceptions of racism among international students of color during COVID-19. *Journal of Diversity in Higher Education, 16*(3), 284–296. https://doi.org/10.1037/dhe0000343

Kushnir, I., & Nunes, A. (2022). Education and the UN development goals projects (MDGs and SDGs): Definitions, links, operationalisations. *Journal of Research in International Education, 21*(1), 3–21. https://doi.org/10.1177/14752409221088942

Lee, C. S. (2019). Global linguistic capital, global cultural capital: International student migrants in China's two-track international education market. *International Journal of Educational Development, 67*, 94–102. https://doi.org/10.1016/j.ijedudev.2019.03.001

Lee, J. J. (2017). Neo-nationalism in higher education: Case of South Africa. *Studies in Higher Education, 42*(5), 869–886. https://doi.org/10.1080/03075079.2017.1293875

Lee, J. J., & Sehoole, C. (2015). Regional, continental, and global mobility to an emerging economy: The case of South Africa. *Higher Education, 70*, 827–843. https://doi.org/10.1007/s10734-015-9869-7

Lipura, S. J., & Collins, F. L. (2020). Towards an integrative understanding of contemporary educational mobilities: A critical agenda for international student mobilities research. *Globalisation, Societies and Education, 18*(3), 343–359. https://doi.org/10.1080/14767724.2020.1711710

Lörz, M., Netz, N. & Quast, H. (2016). Why do students from underprivileged families less often intend to study abroad? *Higher Education, 72*, 153–174. https://doi.org/10.1007/s10734-015-9943-1

Ma, Y., & Pan, S. (2015). Chinese returnees from overseas study: An understanding of brain gain and brain circulation in the age of globalization. *Frontiers of Education in China, 10*(2), 306–329. https://doi.org/10.1007/BF03397067

Martini, E. (2021). Intercultural education: Bring together pluralism and diversity. *Athens Journal of Social Sciences, 8*(1), 31–44. https://doi.org/10.30958/ajss.8-1-2

Mbithi, P. M. F., Mbau, J. S., Muthama, N. J., Inyega, H., & Kalai, J. M. (2021). Higher education and skills development in Africa: An analytical paper on the role of higher learning institutions on sustainable development. *Journal of Sustainability, Environment and Peace, 4*(2), 58–73. https://doi.org/10.53537/JSEP.2021.08.001

McMahon, M. E. (1992). Higher education in a world market: An historical look at the global context of international study. *Higher Education, 24*, 465–482. https://doi.org/10.1007/BF00137243

McMahon, W. W. (2009). *Higher learning, greater good: The private & social benefits of higher education*. The Johns Hopkins University Press. ISBN-10: 0-8018-9053-5.

McNess, E., Arthur, L., & Crossley, M. (2015). 'Ethnographic dazzle' and the construction of the 'Other': Revisiting dimensions of insider and outsider research for international and comparative education. *Compare: A Journal of Comparative and International Education, 45*(2), 295–316. https://doi.org/10.1080/03057925.2013.854616

Morley, L., Alexiadou, N., Garaz, S., González-Monteagudo, J., & Taba, M. (2018). Internationalisation and migrant academics: The hidden narratives of mobility. *Higher Education, 76*, 537–554. https://doi.org/10.1007/s10734-017-0224-z

Mosler Vidal, E., & Laczko, F. (2022). *Migration and the SDGs: Measuring progress – An edited volume*. International Organization for Migration (IOM).

Mulvey, B. (2021). Conceptualizing the discourse of student mobility between 'periphery' and 'semi-periphery': The case of Africa and China. *Higher Education, 81*(3), 437–451. https://doi.org/10.1007/s10734-020-00549-8

Nicolai, S., Wales, J., & Aiazzi, E. (2017). *Education, migration and the 2030 agenda for sustainable development*. Overseas Development Institute. Retrieved September 3, 2023, from http://www.jstor.org/stable/resrep49893

Olowookere, J. K., Olanipekun, W. D., Sokunbi, G. M., & Aderemi, T. A. (2022). Human capital development and sustainable development: Evidence from Nigeria. *Studia Universitatis Babes-Bolyai Oeconomica, 67*(1), 63–76. https://doi.org/10.2478/subboec-2022-0005

Organisation for Economic Co-operation and Development (OECD). (2015). *Education at a glance 2015*. OECD Indicators.

Organisation for Economic Co-operation and Development (OECD). (2018). *The resilience of students with an immigrant background: Factors that shape wellbeing*. OECD Reviews of Migrant Education, OECD Publishing. https://doi.org/10.1787/9789264292093-en

Ortiga, Y. Y. (2018). Constructing a global education hub: The unlikely case of Manila. *Discourse: Studies in the Cultural Politics of Education, 39*(5), 767–781. https://doi.org/10.1080/01596306.2018.1448703

Page, A. G., & Chahboun, S. (2019). Emerging empowerment of international students: How international student literature has shifted to include the students' voices. *Higher Education, 78*, 871–885. https://doi.org/10.1007/s10734-019-00375-7

Page, M. J., McKenzie, J. E., Bossuyt, P. M., Boutron, I., Hoffmann, T. C., Mulrow, C. D., Shamseer, L., Tetzlaff, J. M., Akl, E. A., Brennan, S. E., Chou, R., Glanville, J., Grimshaw, J. M., Hróbjartsson, A., Lalu, M. M., Li, T., Loder, E. W., Mayo-Wilson, E., McDonald, S., & Moher, D. (2021). The PRISMA 2020 statement: An updated guideline for reporting systematic reviews. *BMJ, 372*(71), 1–9. https://doi.org/10.1136/bmj.n71

Payab, A. H., Kautish, P., Sharma, R., Siddiqui, A., Mehta, A., & Siddiqui, M. (2023). Does human capital complement sustainable development goals? Evidence from leading carbon emitter countries. *Utilities Policy, 81*, 101509. https://doi.org/10.1016/j.jup.2023.101509

Perez-Encinas, A., Rodriguez-Pomeda, J., & de Wit, H. (2021). Factors influencing student mobility: A comparative European study. *Studies in Higher Education, 46*(12), 2528–2541. https://doi.org/10.1080/03075079.2020.1725873

PRISMA Flowchart. (2020). Retrieved June 21, 2023, from http://www.prisma-statement.org/

Ramia, G. (2021). Crises in international education, and government responses: A comparative analysis of racial discrimination and violence towards international students. *Higher Education, 82*, 599–613. https://doi.org/10.1007/s10734-021-00684-w

Rao, N. (2010). Migration, education and socio-economic mobility. *Compare: A Journal of Comparative and International Education, 40*(2), 137–145. https://doi.org/10.1080/03057920903545973

Rees, P. (2009). Demography. In R. Kitchin & N. Thrift (Eds.), *International encyclopedia of human geography* (pp. 75–90). Elsevier. https://doi.org/10.1016/B978-008044910-4.00815-4

Sachs, J. D., Kroll, C., Lafortune, G., Fuller, G., & Woelm, F. (2022). *Sustainable development report 2022*. Cambridge University Press. https://doi.org/10.1017/9781009210058

Sidhu, R., & Ishikawa, M. (2022). Destined for Asia: Hospitality and emotions in international student mobilities. *Compare: A Journal of Comparative and International Education, 52*(3), 399–417. https://doi.org/10.1080/03057925.2020.1771544

Sidhu, R., Yeoh, B., & Chang, S. (2015). A situated analysis of global knowledge networks: Capital accumulation strategies of transnationally mobile scientists in Singapore. *Higher Education, 69*, 79–101. https://doi.org/10.1007/s10734-014-9762-9

Sironi, A., Bauloz, C., & Emmanuel, M. (Eds.). (2019). *Glossary on migration*. International Migration Law No. 34. International Organization for Migration (IOM).

Skeldon, R. (2018). *International migration, internal migration, mobility and urbanization*. United Nations. https://www.un-ilibrary.org/content/books/9789210474375

Smith, R. A., & Khawaja, N. G. (2011). A review of the acculturation experiences of international students. *International Journal of Intercultural Relations, 35*(6), 699–713. https://doi.org/10.1016/j.ijintrel.2011.08.004

Souto-Otero, M., Huisman, J., Beerkens, M., De Wit, H., & Vujic, S. (2013). Barriers to international student mobility evidence from the Erasmus Programme. *Educational Researcher, 42*(2), 70–77. https://doi.org/10.3102/0013189X12466696

Stoessel, K., Ihme, T. A., Barbarino, M. L., Fisseler, B., & Stürmer, S. (2015). Sociodemographic diversity and distance education: Who drops out from academic programs and why? *Research in Higher Education, 56*, 228–246. https://doi.org/10.1007/s11162-014-9343-x

Suárez-Orozco, C., Gaytán, F. X., Bang, H. J., Pakes, J., O'Connor, E., & Rhodes, J. (2010). Academic trajectories of newcomer immigrant youth. *Developmental Psychology, 46*(3), 602–618. https://doi.org/10.1037/a0018201

Suárez-Orozco, C., Rhodes, J., & Milburn, M. (2009). Unraveling the immigrant paradox: Academic engagement and disengagement among recently arrived immigrant youth. *Youth\& Society, 41*(2), 151–185. https://doi.org/10.1177/0044118X09333647

Suárez-Orozco, M. M., & Qin-Hilliard, D. B. (2004). *Globalization: Culture and education in the new millennium*. University of California Press. ISBN 0-520-24125-8.

Sutrisno, A., & Pillay, H. (2015). Knowledge transfer through a transnational program partnership between Indonesian and Australian universities. *Asia Pacific Education Review, 16*, 379–388. https://doi.org/10.1007/s12564-015-9384-7

The World Commission on Environment and Development. (1987). *Report of the World Commission on Environment and Development – Our common future*. Retrieved September 4, 2023, from https://sustainabledevelopment.un.org/milestones/wced

Ugnich, E., Chernokozov, A., & Ugnich, M. (2021). Human capital in the system of sustainable development goals: Significance and prospects. *E3S Web Conference, 258*, 7053. https://doi.org/10.1051/e3sconf/202125807053

Umansky, I. M. (2016). To be or not to be EL: An examination of the impact of classifying students as English learners. *Educational Evaluation and Policy Analysis, 38*(4), 714–737. https://doi.org/10.3102/0162373716664802

UNESCO Institute for Lifelong Learning (UIL). (2023). *Lifelong learning*. Retrieved November 11, 2023, from https://www.uil.unesco.org/en/unesco-institute/mandate/lifelong-learning

United Nations (UN). (2023). *Sustainable development goals fast facts-what is sustainable development?* Retrieved September 10, 2023, from https://www.un.org/sustainabledevelopment/blog/2023/08/what-is-sustainable-development/

United Nations Development Programme (UNDP). (2022). *Human development report 2021–2022*. Retrieved July 24, 2023, from https://hdr.undp.org/system/files/documents/global-report-document/hdr2021-22pdf_1.pdf

United Nations Educational, Scientific and Cultural Organization (UNESCO). (2020). *Global education monitoring report 2020: Inclusion and education: All means all* (3rd ed.). UNESCO Publishing.

United Nations General Assembly. (2015). *Transforming our world: The 2030 agenda for sustainable development*. Retrieved September 4, 2023, from https://documents-dds-ny.un.org/doc/UNDOC/GEN/N15/291/89/PDF/N1529189.pdf?OpenElement

Waters, J. L. (2018). International education is political! Exploring the politics of international student mobilities. *Journal of International Students, 8*(3), 1459–1478. https://doi.org/10.32674/jis.v8i3.66

Wen, W., & Hu, D. (2019). The emergence of a regional education hub: Rationales of international students' choice of China as the study destination. *Journal of Studies in International Education, 23*(3), 303–325. https://doi.org/10.1177/1028315318797154

World Bank. (2023). *Human capital project*. Retrieved November 11, 2023, from https://www.worldbank.org/en/publication/human-capital.

Xu, C. L., & Montgomery, C. (2019). Educating China on the move: A typology of contemporary Chinese higher education mobilities. *Review of Education, 7*(3), 598–627. https://doi.org/10.1002/rev3.3139

Yang Hansen, K., & Gustafsson, J. E. (2016). Causes of educational segregation in Sweden–school choice or residential segregation. *Educational Research and Evaluation, 22*(1–2), 23–44. https://doi.org/10.1080/13803611.2016.1178589

Yang, P. (2018). Compromise and complicity in international student mobility: The ethnographic case of Indian medical students at a Chinese university. *Discourse: Studies in the Cultural Politics of Education, 39*(5), 694–708. https://doi.org/10.1080/01596306.2018.1435600

Yang, P. (2020). Toward a framework for (re) thinking the ethics and politics of international student mobility. *Journal of Studies in International Education, 24*(5), 518–534. https://doi.org/10.1177/1028315319889891

Yang, P. (2022). China in the global field of international student mobility: An analysis of economic, human and symbolic capitals. *Compare: A Journal of Comparative and International Education, 52*(2), 308–326. https://doi.org/10.1080/03057925.2020.1764334

Yu, B., Mak, A. S., & Bodycott, P. (2021). Psychological and academic adaptation of mainland Chinese students in Hong Kong universities. *Studies in Higher Education, 46*(8), 1552–1564. https://doi.org/10.1080/03075079.2019.1693991

Yu, B., & Zhang, K. (2016). 'It's more foreign than a foreign country': Adaptation and experience of Mainland Chinese students in Hong Kong. *Tertiary Education and Management, 22*(4), 300–315. https://doi.org/10.1080/13583883.2016.1226944

Yue, Y., & Lu, J. (2022). International students' motivation to study abroad: An empirical study based on expectancy-value theory and self-determination theory. *Frontiers in Psychology, 13*, 1664–1078. https://doi.org/10.3389/fpsyg.2022.841122

Zupic, I., & Čater, T. (2015). Bibliometric methods in management and organization. *Organizational Research Methods, 18*(3), 429–472. https://doi.org/10.1177/1094428114562629

Part IV

Chapter 7

The Potential of Teacher–Student Communicative Action to Overcome the Repercussions of Global Crises

Jennifer Swinehart

American School of Bombay, India

Abstract

Globally, teachers are operating in environments influenced by past, current and anticipated crises. Students today need to develop the critical skills that will empower them to be agents of change in response to these crises. Education for global citizenship offers an approach that can mediate both content and process priorities, yet many teachers do not have the tools and strategies needed to deliver these dual outcomes. Habermas' theory of communicative action offers a framework through which teachers can harness the potential of the so-called *learning lifeworld* to educate for global citizenship. This is of particular importance when considering education through the lens of international sustainable development. The contextualisation of communicative acts within the learning lifeworld offers the prospect of elevating students as agentic leaders within their communities. This chapter focuses on and unpacks the concept of education for global citizenship as a key tool for overcoming current crises and positions the theory of communicative action as a viable theoretical framework in the delivery of that concept. The ethnographic case study presented explores students' perspectives on how their learning lifeworlds shape their identities, highlighting the role of culture, society and person in combatting lifeworld colonisation and nurturing global citizens. It finds that the theory of communicative action can be used as a tool to help students develop

---

Education and Sustainable Development in the Context of Crises:
International Case Studies of Transformational Change, 109–124
Copyright © 2025 by Jennifer Swinehart. Published by Emerald Publishing Limited.
These works are published under the Creative Commons Attribution (CC BY 4.0) licence. Anyone may reproduce, distribute, translate and create derivative works of these works (for both commercial and non-commercial purposes), subject to full attribution to the original publication and authors. The full terms of this licence may be seen at http://creativecommons.org/licences/by/4.0/legalcode
doi:10.1108/978-1-83797-773-420241007

self-directedness and independence. It is argued teachers can use communicative acts to promote and model the values of education for global citizenship, ultimately better preparing today's students for tomorrow's world.

Keywords: Habermas; lifeworld; communicative action; education for global citizenship; ethnographic framework

7.1 Education for Global Citizenship: A Brief Background

Before detailing Habermas' theory of communicative action and its use as a framework for exploring how learning lifeworlds shape students' identities as global citizens, it will first be helpful to establish the context of global citizenship in this chapter. In the current educational context, crises sit central to the experiences of both teachers and students alike. In the last few years alone, disruptions related to climate change, political unrest, international conflicts, technological developments and a global pandemic have demanded that we revisit the purpose of schooling and what an education means for children today. While each of these crises might be attributed to the priorities inherent in past educational models, it is recognised that educational systems which prioritise education for global citizenship, and in particular citizenship education, might provide the best opportunity to overcome these challenges.

Kushnir and Nunes (2022) identify education as the location of soft power in the debate around global sustainability education, as it seems to be key in achieving the sustainable development goals (SDGs) identified by the United Nations. Despite the difficulty in defining what is meant by education, education is explicitly and implicitly embedded in the SDGs and viewed as critical to the global success towards these goals by their 2030 deadline. By arguing that international policymakers ought to combine their efforts to 'promote a world consensus around the meaning of the scope of education and its potential for development, and to work out more practical ways in which education can support and facilitate sustainable development', Kushnir and Nunes (2022, p. 16) underscore the need for both theoretical and practical action in the educational sector towards sustainable development.

The challenge Kushnir and Nunes (2022) raise with regard to the lack of a singular definition of education in the context of sustainable development holds true for the definition of education for global citizenship more specifically. Estellés and Fischman (2020, p. 3) explain that it is 'frequently presented as the result of a simple evolutionary pedagogical model, that is, the latest, best, and most comprehensive model that incorporates all the positive goals and practices from previous efforts … and overcome their limitations'. Both pairs of authors call attention to the complexity and multifaceted nature of global citizenship, one that continues to evolve over time.

Mannion et al. (2011) refer to the increasing focus on globally orientated pedagogical models and curricula as a set of key concepts without offering a singular definition. Table 7.1 presents key aspects of three sub-fields they identify within

Table 7.1. Based on Key Aspects of the Education for Global Citizenship Sub-fields as Identified by Mannion et al. (2011).

Environmental Education	Development Education	Citizenship Education
• Conservation and environmental education • Sustainability studies • Ecological and nature studies • Human–environmental relationships	• Education for sustainable development • Third world studies • Global education • Globalisation • Peace education • Social justice and overcoming inequity	• Justice and democracy • Civic responsibility and civic studies • Private sphere as political • Entrepreneurial education • International education

the umbrella concept of education for global citizenship: environmental education, development education and citizenship education.

Their analysis, synthesised above, includes both a lineage of how each sub-field generally originated as well as commentary on the points of intersection across all three sub-fields. Together, these sub-fields have both historical and contemporary influences on the broader concept of education for global citizenship used today.

At one time, education for global citizenship was critiqued as an education exclusively for the elite (see Drerup, 2020; Estellés & Fischman, 2020). International schools that were founded to provide a Western-style education to the children of internationally mobile parents increasingly cater to both expatriate and local families who want their children to be educated in ideologies characterised by individualism, freedom, democracy, egalitarianism, rationalism, optimism and/or universalism (Tate, 2016). Originally created to serve students in international schools, the International Baccalaureate Organisation (IBO) offers four programmes, at least one of which is implemented in over 5,700 schools in 160 countries worldwide (IBO, 2024). The IBO mission 'aims to develop inquiring, knowledgeable and caring young people who help to create a better and more peaceful world through intercultural understanding and respect' (IBO, 2019), and each of its programmes focuses on nurturing global perspectives, international mindedness and independent learners (Hill, 2003; Storz & Hoffman, 2018).

Drerup (2020) offers an argument for a universal application of global citizenship education as one that is worthwhile and worthy for all learners. While he acknowledges some of the difficulties with global citizenship education as one originally reserved for the elite, he states that this conflation of genesis and application is wrong: global citizenship education 'should not be identified with an elite education, but understood as a means of combatting global educational, economic and political injustices, among others, in the form of a general education, *also* of the elites' (Drerup, 2020, p. 37). Thus, it is imperative that educators today can provide an education for global citizenship that addresses both the content and skills their students will need now and into the future.

In both national (Mannion et al., 2011) and international (Gardner-McTaggart, 2018; Hayden & Thompson, 2016) school systems, education for global citizenship has become increasingly central in the development of curriculum objectives and the articulation of learner outcomes. This approach can serve as a mechanism for providing students with the knowledge, skills and dispositions they might need to engage with global issues (Mannion et al., 2011). An increased focus on cognitive, metacognitive and affective skill instruction and development is recognised as particularly crucial to a holistic, future-focused education that prepares students for an uncertain future (Häkkinen et al, 2016; Li, 2012; Organisation for Economic Cooperation and Development (OECD), 2018; van de Oudeweetering & Voogt, 2017). In order to reach their potential, students must be supported to apply cognitive skills in increasingly complex and unfamiliar scenarios (Pellegrino, 2017). Funke et al. (2017) recognise the connection between knowledge and problem-solving and reiterate that the teaching of cognitive competencies is an essential element of preparing students to solve the problems they will face well into the 21st century.

This focus on what students will need to overcome crises, as opposed to reproducing past mistakes, is essential for teachers today. Mannion et al. (2011, p. 452) argue that there is '… a need to work critically and creatively at new ways of "doing" education that respond adequately to the new condition of citizenship in a global context'. Estellés and Fischman (2020) speak to the impact of an increased focus on education for global citizenship on teacher training programmes, cautioning that an oversimplification of what it means to be a productive citizen can erode the effectiveness of teachers in being able to deliver authentic and meaningful learning experiences to their students. Considering the three gifts of teaching offered by Biesta (2021), that teaching gives the learner something they did not ask for, that learners develop knowledge within the scope of their current understanding as well the skills to access understanding that is not yet known and that learners gain insights into themselves as learners, it is essential to support teachers is giving these gifts through the lens of education for global citizenship.

7.2 Applying Habermas' Theory of Communicative Action to Address a Gap in Educating for Global Citizenship

To understand the potential of communicative action as a resource in educating for global citizenship, it is important to first understand the purpose and structure of the theory. In the theory of communicative action, Habermas (1984, 1987) presents a social theory that outlines how an individual comes to understand the social world through linguistic communication. He suggests that speech is used to coordinate action, and that people reach consensus on their interpretations of their shared world through language. Two aspects of rationality are essential to the process of making meaning: communicative reality, which is achieved when an individual reaches 'an understanding about something in the world with at least one other participant' (Habermas, 1984, p. 11), and purposive-rational action, when an individual's choice '*ends* from a clearly articulated horizon of *values* and organizes suitable *means* in consideration of alternative *consequences*' (Habermas, 1984, p. 281). These two aspects of rationality work in tandem to help an individual engage with and make meaning about their lifeworld.

Habermas refers to three purposes, or validity claims, behind a linguistic act: a validity claim to truth, rightness and truthfulness (1984, 1987). Validity claims are inherent in speech acts and have moral, rational and practical implications for the social order established within a lifeworld (Finlayson, 2005). Essential to the notion of creating democratic societies, validity claims establish an expectation that individuals can and should assert their perspectives and engage as legitimate participants within democratic processes (Moran & Murphy, 2011; von Ahlefeld Nisser, 2017). Ultimately, these validity claims also contribute to the formation of self-awareness through communication, positioning an individual to build self-determination and self-realisation as a legitimate stakeholder within their lifeworld.

While the outcome of ego-identity is an independent action, identity formation is initially social. Habermas (1984, p. 58) explains that '[i]ndividuals owe their identities as persons exclusively to their identification with, or internalization of, features of collective identity; personal identity is a mirror image of collective identity'. This suggests that within a school context, ego development is social before becoming an autonomous process, thus shifting from external to internal. In order to process the influences of teachers, peers and wider community norms, learners must be able to recognise and adapt to all that influences their development, particularly the role of their learning lifeworld.

The process of communicative action and the development of ego-identity takes place within the lifeworld, which forms the boundary for individuals to equitably engage in communicative acts to reach mutual understanding (Habermas, 1984, 1987). This is where speaker and listener come together in 'a context that, itself boundless, draws boundaries' around those participating in the exchange (Habermas, 1987, p. 132). A desire to both understand and be understood implies positive presupposition, and Habermas frames these exchanges as ones in which the lifeworld members should feel empowered to share their perspectives openly and confidently as equals; within the lifeworld, it is 'everyone's right to state their opinions and values based on their experience and knowledge and everyone's willingness to speak in an understandable way' (von Ahlefeld Nisser, 2017, p. 875). This therefore assumes that lifeworld participants engage in these acts sincerely and with good intention.

The lifeworld consists of three components – culture, society and person – each of which is essential within the act of communication (Habermas, 1984, 1987). Culture is the broadest designation, and it provides community members with the necessary knowledge to develop understandings about the lifeworld and beyond. It includes a community's values, traditions and norms as well as the beliefs inherent in commonly used language (Deakin Crick & Joldersma, 2006; MacNeil et al., 2009). School cultures serve as the 'normative glue that holds a particular school together … steering people in a common direction' (Sergiovanni, 2000, p. 14), shaping patterns of interaction between individuals across the community. Society is a smaller group within a lifeworld that members associate with over time, either by choice or by design. Yelland et al. (2020, p. 1) suggest that '[a] dynamic education system forms part of this ecosystem, both producing and attracting participations and creating aspirational opportunities for citizens that are flexible and globally focussed'. This function of school as society is a key influence on the development of student ego-identities within a learning community. Person is every individual within a lifeworld, each of whom has the capacity to speak and act such that they ultimately develop their ego-identity. These communicative experiences are what give an individual the potential to develop an understanding of the world and of themself. Gosling (2000, p. 296) cites Habermas to both acknowledge autonomy and responsibility as key outcomes of an education and caution that, 'to be successful, educational practices must permit and encourage forms of communication which are not distorted by imbalances of power or other blocks to open and rational discussion'. Habermas argues for cultural, societal and personal engagements that are equitable and driven by a desire to understand. The interconnectivity of the lifeworld structures forms the foundation for learning as a social experience and 'becomes a necessary condition for learning because it is the most valid way for producing knowledge, examining the validity of existing knowledge, and providing opportunities for acquiring contextually useful knowledge for each citizen' (Regmi, 2020, p. 225). This pattern of engagement across the three lifeworld elements is reproduced within each lifeworld and is also transferable to other lifeworlds.

In contrast to the lifeworld, Habermas (1987) presents the system as a competing space that shapes identity formation. The system is the 'aspect of society where imperatives of technical efficiency and bureaucracy have precedence' (Murphy, 2009, p. 82) as the influencers of societal and individual development. In our modern age, money and power wield most influence over culture, society and individuation with the intention of furthering capitalist priorities at the expense of individual decision-making and independence. As a self-sustaining and self-replicating phenomenon, the lifeworld is maintained through communicative actions; in contrast, the system is maintained through the meaning made within the lifeworld (Habermas, 1987). This relationship is parasitic, as the system exists within the lifeworld and relies on the lifeworld's cultural and societal pillars to survive. Habermas conceptualises the notion that in order to reinforce the hierarchy of lifeworld over system, patterns of communicative action must be prioritised over patterns of instrumental action. Even so, he recognises that the system is an increasingly powerful threat to the lifeworld (Habermas, 1987). Finlayson (2005) explains that the system benefits from the redirection of decision-making away from the lifeworld and the shifting of agency from the individual to systemic authorities. When this happens, the intention of mutual understanding inherent in communicative acts is no longer present (Habermas, 1987). Regmi (2020, p. 224) specifies that 'when the three components of the lifeworld are not mediated by communicative actions the lifeworld becomes incapable for performing the three basic functions of the lifeworld'.

For schools, bureaucratic structures, political intrusion and external threats due to crises can be seen as system threats to the learning lifeworld. By directly addressing the threat of colonisation in education, Habermas underscores the important role of schools to keep learning focused on lifeworld-nourishing priorities. He goes on to address the potential hazard of the system for teachers, citing threats that could erode the freedom and independence practitioners need to meet to provide dynamic learning experiences for students. The threat posed by the system colonising the lifeworld is great, thus the uncoupling of the system from the lifeworld is of particular importance (Habermas, 1987). Parkin (1996, p. 423) recognises how ordinary communicative interactions can result in extraordinary outcomes, such as the establishing and reproducing of patterns of belief, of consent and legitimacy, of status and identity, and of perception', reinforcing the importance and value of communicative action in the classroom. Within the context of education for global citizenship, system threats that stem from the priorities of exploitative actors could ultimately perpetuate and even amplify the negative outcomes of crises. For teachers to be able to withstand the colonising threats of the system, they must have the competencies and skills to positively leverage the elements of the lifeworld through communicative acts. This reiterates the importance and value of communicative action as a means for combatting system colonisation and securing the reproduction of the lifeworld within the educational setting.

As young people prepare to engage with a world ravaged by current and potential crises, considering how educational models can actively combat this colonisation and preserve the lifeworld will be of critical importance for the future. A review of the literature suggests that the application of the theory of communicative action in education can serve to protect the lifeworld and stave off the threats of the system through its support of citizenship education, well-being and holistic education and self-directed learning (see, for example, Cherryholmes, 1981; Deakin Crick & Joldersma, 2006; Ewert, 1991; Fleming & Murphy, 2010; Lovat, 2013; Mezirow, 1985; Regmi, 2017). Fleming and Murphy's (2010, p. 203) assertion that '[e]ducation has the task of ensuring that democratic skills and processes are handed on from one generation to the next' implores us to think carefully and seriously about the scope of Habermas' influence on educating for a democratic future.

While some research has shown how the theory of communicative action can be used to support education for global citizenship, the perspectives of students as the perceived beneficiaries of communicative acts have not been researched. The originality of this chapter is therefore in surfacing the voices of students through an ethnographic case study designed to explore the influence of their learning lifeworlds on the development of their ego-identities as individuals.

7.3 Methodology

The gaps in prior research about how students perceive the development of their ego-identities in their learning lifeworlds prompted me to seek answers to how the theory of communicative action could be an effective tool in educating for global citizenship. A fundamental question this gap surfaces hinges on the construct of communicative action and its potential to transform students into active and engaged global citizens who can overcome persisting repercussions of the impact of crises on their generation: *How might the theory of communicative action serve as a vehicle for developing student self-directedness and independence as facets of education for global citizenship?*

Using Habermas' theory of communicative action as my theoretical framework, I designed an ethnographic case study that would seek out student perspectives on their learning lifeworlds and engage them in the creation of knowledge through communicative action. This methodology allowed for the generation of data that could be used to explore the relationships between data sets as well as accommodate the study of theory in a real-world setting (Fusch et al., 2017). Designing an ethnographic case study aligned with the use of Habermas' theory of communicative action as through their involvement, participants had the opportunity to define the realities of their lifeworld experiences.

The research site was an international school in Hong Kong offering the International Baccalaureate Primary Years (IBPYP), Middle Years (IBMYP) and Diploma (IBDP) Programmes. As referenced earlier in this chapter, these IB programmes seek to support students in becoming internationally minded and develop skills to prepare them for an uncertain future (see Häkkinen et al., 2016; IBO, 2019; Li, 2012; OECD, 2018; van de Oudeweetering & Voogt, 2017). I was particularly interested in exploring student experiences within the IBMYP to better understand how this framework influenced student learning lifeworlds. Taking place over two phases, the study included 136 IBMYP students in Grades 6 and 10. The grade levels that were selected were the first and last ones in the IBMYP, thus allowing for the exploration of ego-identity development at different stages of student learning journeys.

The mixed-methods approach of using questionnaires and interviews as the tools for data generation allowed for a larger number of student perspectives to be solicited and were designed to generate both quantitative and qualitative data. All 136 participants completed the questionnaire, which itself included both quantitative and qualitative elements: respondents rated responses to some questions using a Likert scale, and some questions provided additional opportunities to include open-ended responses. Twelve students opted to participate in a semi-structured interview designed to function as a communicative act that 'presupposes language as the medium for a kind of reaching understanding, in the course of which participants, through relating to a world, reciprocally raise validity claims that can be accepted or contested' (Habermas, 1984, p. 99). In the process of data generation, communicative action served as a driver for how equity through mutual understanding could be elevated.

The qualitative data generated through the questionnaires and interviews were analysed following Braun and Clarke's (2006, 2022) guidelines for thematic analysis. Their six-step process provides a flexible and methodologically sound approach to qualitative data analysis, which includes researcher immersion in the data, generation of initial codes, identification of themes, review of themes, definition and naming of themes and publication of findings. Drawing on this approach, I leveraged my identity as an ethnographer to emphasise what Braun and Clarke describe as the 'inevitable subjectivity of data coding and analysis, and the researcher's active role in coding and theme generation' (2022, p. 8). Through reflexive thematic analysis, I framed my engagement with the data through the theory of communicative action and used the pillars of the lifeworld as the organising concept for my analysis. The centrality of Habermas' theory in my study led me to decide on and develop themes I identified as relevant to the case location of an international school offering the IBMYP, holding value in relation to the lifeworld elements of culture, society and person and representative of the literature related to education for global citizenship. The intention in the following sections is to present the value of these themes through the lens of communicative action to support individual teachers, school leaders and policymakers in future application or further exploration.

7.4 The Impact of the Lifeworld on Student Self-Directedness and Independence

This section presents the findings from the ethnographic case study exploring student perspectives on their learning lifeworlds. The discussion below highlights the critical role of the lifeworld elements of culture, society and person in resisting colonisation by the system; this area of focus is emphasised as it provides a justification for communicative acts as a mechanism for delivering an education for global citizenship that prepares students to overcome the challenges of crises.

7.5 Student Self-Directedness and Independence

Education for global citizenship strives to create learning environments in which students can monitor their own capabilities with increasing independence. Biesta (2020, 2008) identifies qualification as one key function and outcome of education, that is to provide students with the knowledge, skills, understandings, dispositions and critical thinking skills they will need to operate in the world. In addition to the responsibility of schooling to provide direction and motivation, Ryan and Deci (2020) reiterate the need for self-determined learning experiences, through which teachers can encourage students to become more intrinsically motivated and strengthen their investment in their own learning.

In this study, participants reflected on their familiarity with and use of 13 skill subsets included in the IBMYP framework referred to as approaches to learning (ATL) skills. Over 50% of respondents reported familiarity with self-management, organisation, reflection, research, creative thinking and communication skills, and over 75% highlighted self-management and communication as skills they recognised. As a framework designed to deliver a holistic education that teaches global mindedness, the IBMYP has identified these as skills core to its programme, reiterating their importance for an education for global citizenship.

In both the questionnaire and interview responses, students identified both strengths and areas for growth for themselves as learners as they relate to ATL skills. The following illustrative quotes show how students were reflective about their own capabilities as learners, a key facet of ego-identity development within their learning lifeworlds:

> At times I get a bit confused and frustrated and ... I have been pushed out of my comfort zone, but a personal goal of mine is to take opportunities to do things that are out of my comfort zone, get

over my fears and ... I have been able to do things I couldn't before which will help me achieve hopefully great things in the future.

I think [I have improved in] organisation, because I've become a bit more organised with my work. And even if I tell my parents I don't have homework it's because I don't want them to worry and I know I could do it in my own time. Without them pestering me and telling me to be organised because I know how to do it – I know how to be organised, but sometimes it's just a little hard.

If you learn something on your own or you work on it by yourself, ... you remember it better .... The feeling of anxiety and, 'Oh my gosh, I have this huge project to do' ... it's almost part of it. I feel like working on your own and creating your own project, managing yourself and researching and thinking, organising, those are all the ATL skills, but you do them by yourself. And that way it's more independent. You create a better piece at the end, because you've done all this stuff and you understand it better.

These students are able to identify the impacts of their learning lifeworld on their development, reflecting the findings of Jeno and Diseth (2014) that through authentic learning experiences, students find relevance and become more self-determined. Their comments are indicative of students who are both intrinsically and extrinsically motivated to develop their skills as learners, skills that will be essential for them as they become the workers and leaders of tomorrow.

7.6 Withstanding the Threat of System Colonisation

As the domain of interactions characterised by open, authentic and rational discourse (Habermas, 1984, 1987), the lifeworld has the potential to situate space in which education for global citizenship can thrive. Individuals can build shared understanding and foster mutual recognition through communicative acts in which they treat each other as equals. In contrast, the system is composed of societal elements that disempower the individual. Markets, political apparati and oppressive structures instead determine and drive the types of exchanges that take place in the system. Habermas (1987) goes so far as to suggest that system colonisation can infringe upon the basic human rights of students. In order to deliver an education for global citizenship, teachers need to be able to perpetuate the lifeworld and stave off the threat of the system.

In both academic and social-emotional realms, the influence of teachers on student development is palpable. In their four dimensions of teacher effectiveness, Stronge et al. (2011) highlight both craft and environment as essential to teacher success. The learning lifeworld of each student will be impacted directly by the content and the processes delivered by their teacher. In this study, over 40% of respondents identified factors related to inclusivity and safety as being important to their learning, with 31 alluding to fun and 23 to confidence as either positive or negative impacts on their learning. Those who responded positively spoke about working in their comfort zones, feeling relaxed, receiving help, being with friends and having independence and choice as beneficial factors in their experiences.

The illustrative quotes that follow demonstrate what some participants identified as the specific ways in which teachers shaped their learning lifeworlds:

> Everyone's very helpful in trying to help you specifically grow ... Everyone's pretty selfless in helping you develop in your own way, in your journey ... [Teachers] are helpful in the way that they're able to ... get you to do the best that they can, by being critical on yourself and thinking 'hey, maybe I can refine this' and going through multiple, multiple drafts and doing them with you as well.

> It's nice, and the people ... they're really nice, and there's a lot of things to learn ... It's very different from my other school because there's more people and they're a lot nicer ... and you get to learn a lot more ... than some other schools.

> Our teachers have always pushed us to go beyond ourselves ... they ask us to first identify how do we connect with something. And how does it connect to us. And then from there, they really try to get us to go beyond into the ... wider world.

These quotes reiterate how critical a teacher's role is in setting the cultural tone in the learning lifeworld and the direct impact a teacher's approach has on student learning. This suggests that students valued the support they received for being able to work towards goals that had meaning to them personally and were crafted to align with their own strengths and areas for growth as a learner.

As teachers directly influence school culture and student learning (see, for example, Deakin Crick & Joldersma, 2006; Sergiovanni, 2000; Stronge et al., 2011), the capacity of a teacher to cultivate dynamic learning environments and contribute to positive school cultures might be curtailed by a colonising system. Milley (2008, p. 67) reiterates that teachers might internalise gaps in programming as personal failures, '... leading to crises of motivation whereby they detach themselves from their academic identities, educational endeavours, or the labour market'. These are all fundamental threats posed by the colonisation of the lifeworld. A loss of meaning, withdrawal of legitimation and crisis in orientation and education could deteriorate teacher purpose and trust in the educational system, adversely impacting students and their learning.

Protecting the lifeworld against colonisation is essential for its survival. Kemmis (1998), Deakin Crick and Joldersma (2006) and Regmi (2017) all consider colonisation of the lifeworld as fundamentally disruptive to achieving the philosophical aims of education. As students experience an education for global citizenship, they are engaging with their immediate learning lifeworld as well as learning the skills to transfer to future lifeworlds. Weinberg (2007, p. 82) anticipates the threat of colonisation when she asks '...what consequences might flow for Habermasian theory if in fact our efforts to sustain the assumption of communicative competence are not just temporarily interrupted but quite simply fail over the long term.' It is imperative that in our efforts to equip students to face and overcome the challenges that lie ahead, communicative acts are used to perpetuate the learning lifeworlds that will best position students to innovate future success.

To this end, the call to action for teachers to embed communicative action into approaches to education for global citizenship is apparent. By seeking to engage students as equal partners through communicative acts, teachers can actively and authentically nurture self-directed and independent learners who understand and value the positive impact they can make within and beyond the classroom. In addressing power through communication, the theory of communicative action recognises the importance of classroom spaces that decrease hierarchy and increase agency in learners. For students to be able to address power dynamics through their own communicative acts, they must first experience what it means to engage in communicative acts that are intended to support participants in reaching mutual understanding within an exchange. The perspectives surfaced through this study indicate that students are aware of when teachers are and are not successfully creating learning environments that foster the skills of global citizenship. In those successful examples, intentional and accessible communicative acts formed a foundation of perpetuating the lifeworld through positive cultural, societal and personal engagements. When teachers can consider the learning lifeworld as a core focus of their instruction, the theory of communicative action and the use of communicative acts can support teachers as they develop and deliver education for global citizenship for their students.

7.7 Conclusion

This chapter has considered the important role education for global citizenship can play in overcoming the repercussions of global crises. Fostering student mindsets that promote self-reflection, self-directedness, responsibility and agency will be essential to prepare them for a volatile, uncertain, complex and ambiguous world (Stein, 2021). Habermas' theory of communicative action has served as a viable framework for leveraging communicative acts to empower teachers in their design and delivery of an education for global citizenship. An ethnographic case study has been used to demonstrate how students see their learning lifeworlds and the role that culture, society and person play in shaping their identities as learners.

This analysis substantiates Habermas' assertion that humans share cultural knowledge, reach mutual understanding and connect to society through language, all key skills in an education designed to address current and future challenges students will face. Drerup (2020, p. 36) impels us to think about the possibility inherent in an education for global citizenship, suggesting that 'it should be clear that the global elite should cultivate the values that are central to GCE, but that CGE, despite many socio-economic obstacles, *can* in principle be taught and practiced in all kinds of educational contexts'. The notion of agency within one's learning lifeworld is something every student deserves, and the results presented in this chapter emphasise the critical role that culture, society and person play in shaping an individual's worldview.

Habermas' theory of communicative action provides a rationale for increasing the opportunities for equitable communicative acts in the curriculum with the intention to nurture student voice and self-directedness (Sarid, 2017). For this to happen, educators must increase the kinds of exchanges that put student and teacher on equal footing in recognition of the viability of each student's lifeworld experiences (Harris, 2019). The classroom environment, and school in general, must become a place where every voice holds value and is respected. If teachers can engage students in authentic and meaningful communicative acts, we stand a better chance of delivering an education for global citizenship that will allow us to serve the needs of learners in particular, and humanity in general, today and in the decades to come. By inviting students themselves to deconstruct the impact of culture, society and person on their experiences as students, this study fills a gap in exploring students' perspectives on the impact of the learning lifeworld in shaping their identities as learners. The results presented in this chapter offer a unique contribution by surfacing student voices to showcase the value of communicative action in developing self-directed and independent global citizens.

References

Biesta, G. (2008). Good education in an age of measurement: On the need to reconnect with the question of purpose in education. *Educational Assessment, Evaluation and Accountability*, *21*(1), 33–46. https://doi.org/10.1007/s11092-008-9064-9

Biesta, G. (2020). Risking ourselves in education: Qualification, socialization, and subjectification revisited. *Educational Theory*, *70*(1), 89–104. https://doi.org/10.1111/edth.12411

Biesta, G. (2021). The three gifts of teaching: Towards a non-ecological future for moral education. *Journal of Moral Education*, *50*(1), 39–54. https://doi.org/10.1080/03057240.2020.1763279

Braun, V., & Clarke, V. (2006). Using thematic analysis in psychology. *Qualitative Research in Psychology*, *3*(2), 77–101. https://doi.org/10.1191/1478088706qp063oa

Braun, V., & Clarke, V. (2022). Conceptual and design thinking for thematic analysis. *Qualitative Psychology*, *9*(1), 3–26. https://doi.org/10.1037/qup0000196

Cherryholmes, C. H. (1981). US social and political education. *Teaching Political Science*, *8*(3), 245–260. https://doi.org/10.1080/00922013.1981.11000236

Deakin Crick, R. E. D., & Joldersma, C. W. (2006). Habermas, lifelong learning and citizenship education. *Studies in Philosophy and Education*, *26*(2), 77–95. https://doi.org/10.1007/s11217006-9015-1

Drerup, J. (2020). Global citizenship education, global educational injustice and the postcolonial critique. *Global Justice: Theory Practice Rhetoric*, *12*(1), 27–54. https://doi.org/10.21248/gjn.12.01.230

Estellés, M., & Fischman, G. E. (2020). Who needs global citizenship education? A review of the literature on teacher education. *Journal of Teacher Education*, *72*(2), 1–14. https://doi.org/10.1177/0022487120920254

Ewert, G. (1991). Habermas and education: A comprehensive overview of the influence of Habermas in educational literature. *Review of Educational Research, 61*(3), 345–378. https://doi.org/10.3102/00346543061003345

Finlayson, J. G. (2005). *Habermas: A very short introduction.* OUP Oxford. ISBN 0-19-284095-9.

Fleming, T., & Murphy, M. (2010). *Habermas, critical theory and education.* Routledge. ISBN 0-203-86489-1.

Funke, J., Fischer, A., & Holt, D. V. (2017). Competencies for complexity: Problem solving in the twenty-first century. In E. Care, P. Griffin, M. Wilson (Eds.), *Educational assessment in an information age* (pp. 41–53). https://doi.org/10.1007/978-3-319-65368-6_3

Fusch, P. I., Fusch, G. E., & Ness, L. R. (2017). How to conduct a mini-ethnographic case study: A guide for novice researchers. *The Qualitative Report, 22*(3), 923–941. http://nsuworks.nova.edu/tqr/vol22/iss3/16

Gardner-McTaggart, A. (2018). Leadership of international schools and the international Baccalaureate learner profile. *Educational Management Administration & Leadership, 47*(5), 766–784. https://doi.org/10.1177/1741143217745883

Gosling, D. (2000). Using Habermas to evaluate two approaches to negotiated assessment. *Assessment & Evaluation in Higher Education, 25*(3), 293–304. https://doi.org/10.1080/02602930050135158

Habermas, J. (1984). *The theory of communicative action: Volume 1: Lifeword and system: A critique of functionalist reason.* Beacon Press.

Habermas, J. (1987). *The theory of communicative action: Volume 2: Lifeword and system: A critique of functionalist reason.* Beacon Press.

Häkkinen, P., Järvelä, S., Mäkitalo-Siegl, K., Ahonen, A., & Valtonen, T. (2016). Preparing teacher-students for twenty-first-century learning practices (PREP 21): A framework for enhancing collaborative problem-solving and strategic learning skills. *Teachers and Teaching: Theory and Practice, 23*(1), 25–41. https://doi.org/10.1080/13540602.2016.1203772

Harris, M. (2019). Habermas, Vattimo and feedback: 'Learning gap' or 'learning journey'? *The Heythrop Journal, 61*(5), 842–851. https://doi.org/10.1111/heyj.13413

Hayden, M., & Thompson, J. (2016). *International schools: Current issues and future prospects.* Symposium Books Ltd. ISBN 978-1-873927-92-2.

Hill, I. (2003). The history of international education: An international Baccalaureate perspective. In M. Hayden, J. Thompson, & G. Walker (Eds.), *International education in practice* (pp. 28–37). Routledge. https://doi.org/10.4324/9780203416983.

International Baccalaureate Organisation. (2019). *MYP: From principles into practice.* International Baccalaureate Organisation.

International Baccalaureate Organisation. (2024). *Facts and figures* [online]. International Baccalaureate Organisation: Benefits. https://www.ibo.org/about-the-ib/facts-andfigures/

Jeno, L. M., & Diseth, Å. (2014). A self-determination theory perspective on autonomy support, autonomous self-regulation, and perceived school performance. *Reflecting Education, 9*(1), 120.

Kemmis, S. (1998). System and lifeworld, and the conditions of learning in late modernity. *Curriculum Studies, 6*(3), 269–305. https://doi.org/10.1080/14681369800200043

Kushnir, I., & Nunes, A. (2022). Education and the UN development goals projects (MDGs and SDGs): Definitions, links, operationalisations. *Journal of Research in International Education, 21*(1), 3–21. https://doi.org/10.1177/14752409221088942

Li, N. (2012). *Approaches to learning: A literature review.* International Baccalaureate Organisation.

Lovat, T. (2013). Jürgen Habermas: Education's reluctant hero. *Social theory and education research* (pp. 81–95). Routledge. ISBN 9780429234293.

MacNeil, A. J., Prater, D. L., & Busch, S. (2009). The effects of school culture and climate on student achievement. *International Journal of Leadership in Education, 12*(1), 73–84. https://doi.org/10.1080/13603120701576241

Mannion, G., Biesta, G., Priestley, M., & Ross, H. (2011). The global dimension in education and education for global citizenship: Genealogy and critique. The political economy of global citizenship education (pp. 134–147). Routledge. https://doi.org/10.4324/9781315540856

Mezirow, J. (1985). A critical theory of self-directed learning. New directions for continuing. *Education, 25*, 17–30.

Milley, P. (2008). On Jürgen Habermas' critical theory and the political dimensions of educational administration. In E. A. Samier & A. G. Stanley (Eds.), *Political approaches to educational administration and leadership* (pp. 54–72). Routledge. ISBN 9780203928677.

Moran, P., & Murphy, M. (2011). Habermas, pupil voice, rationalism, and their meeting with Lacan's Objet Petit A. *Studies in Philosophy and Education, 31*(2), 171–181. https://doi.org/10.1007/s11217-011-9271-6

Murphy, M. (2009). Bureaucracy and its limits: Accountability and rationality in higher education. *British Journal of Sociology of Education, 30*(6), 683–695. https://doi.org/10.1080/01425690903235169

Organisation for Economic Co-operation and Development (OECD). (2018). *The future of education and skills: Education 2030*. OECD Education Working Papers. https://www.oecd.org/education/2030/E2030%20Position%20Paper%20(05.04.2018).pdf

Parkin, A. C. (1996). On the practical relevance of Habermas's theory of communicative action. *Social Theory and Practice, 22*(3), 417-441. https://doi.org/10.5840/soctheorpract199622313

Pellegrino, J. W. (2017). *Teaching, learning and assessing 21st century skills* (pp. 223–251). https://doi.org/10.1787/9789264270695-en

Regmi, K. D. (2017). Habermas, lifeworld and rationality: Towards a comprehensive model of lifelong learning. *International Journal of Lifelong Education, 36*(6), 679–695. https://doi.org/10.1080/02601370.2017.1377776

Regmi, K. D. (2020). Social foundations of lifelong learning: A Habermasian perspective. *International Journal of Lifelong Education, 39*(2), 219–233. https://doi.org/10.1080/02601370.2020.1758813https://doi.org/10.1111/heyj.13413

Ryan, R. M., & Deci, E. L. (2020). Intrinsic and extrinsic motivation from a self-determination theory perspective: Definitions, theory, practices, and future directions. *Contemporary Educational Psychology, 61*, 101860. https://doi.org/10.1016/j.cedpsych.2020.101860

Sarid, A. (2017). Rethinking the modernist curriculum with Habermas's concept of self-critical appropriation. *Journal of Curriculum Studies, 49*(4), 456–475. https://doi.org/10.1080/00220272.2017.1307457

Sergiovanni, T. J. (2000). *The lifeworld of leadership: Creating culture, community, and personal meaning in our schools*. The Jossey-Bass Education Series. ERIC.ISBN-0-7879-5028-9.

Stein, S. (2021). Reimagining global citizenship education for a volatile, uncertain, complex, and ambiguous (VUCA) world. *Globalisation, Societies and Education, 19*(4), 482–495. https://doi.org/10.1080/14767724.2021.1904212

Storz, M., & Hoffman, A. R. (2018). Becoming an international Baccalaureate middle years program: Perspectives of teachers, students, and administrators. *Journal of Advanced Academics, 29*(3), 216–248. https://doi.org/10.1177/1932202X18770171

Stronge, J. H., Ward, T. J., & Grant, L. (2011). What makes good teachers good? A cross-case analysis of the connection between teacher effectiveness and student achievement. *Journal of Teacher Education, 62*(4), 339–355. https://doi.org/10.1177/0022487111404241

Tate, N. (2016). What are international schools for? In M. Hayden & J. Thompson (Eds.), *International schools: Current issues and future prospects*, (pp. 17–36). Symposium. ISBN 978-1-873927-92-2.

van de Oudeweetering, K., & Voogt, J. (2017). *Teachers' voice in the development of 21st century competencies*. https://www.bera.ac.uk/blog/teachers-voice-in-thedevelopment-of-curricula-for-21st-century-competences

von Ahlefeld Nisser, D. (2017). Can collaborative consultation, based on communicative theory, promote an inclusive school culture? *Issues in Educational Research*, *27*(4), 874–891. https://search.informit.org/doi/10.3316/informit.218874271405538

Weinberg, D. (2007). Habermas, rights, and the learning disabled citizen. *Social Theory & Health*, *5*(1), 70–87. https://doi.org/10.1057/palgrave.sth.8700087

Yelland, N., Muspratt, S., Bartholomaeus, C., Karthikeyan, N., Chan, A., Leung, W. M. V., Lee, I., Soo, L. M. J., Lim, K. M., & Saltmarsh, S. (2020). Lifeworlds of nine- and ten-year-old children: Out-of-school activities in three global cities. *Globalisation, Societies and Education*, *19*(3), 259–273. https://doi.org/10.1080/14767724.2020.1816921

Chapter 8

The Inner Development Goals: Changing Educational Systems to Meet the Challenge of Human-Generated Global Crises

Phil Wood

Nottingham Trent University, UK

Abstract

We are facing a number of concurrent human-induced crises which, it might be claimed, are the result of entangled processes which flow between and through the issues of climate change, environmental degradation, political instability, global health problems and economic inequalities. These crises are now posing existential threats to ecosystems, habitats, lifeforms and humans. One reaction to these crises has been the instigation of the sustainable development goals (SDGs). Their influence can be argued to have met varied levels of impact and success, but in a complex, interconnected world, perhaps, it is too much to expect that they would, by themselves, act as a management tool which would solve all our ills as they focus on the large scale, not the individual. This leaves a gap for a framework which supports individual growth towards supporting sustainability. The inner development goals (IDGs, 2021) framework is a recent innovation, initially suggested by three Swedish organisations with the express intent of fostering capacities and perspectives at the individual level which will encourage populations to engage with the crises we face in more informed, motivated and practical ways. Through an engagement with the literature, this chapter considers the need for the IDGs in education as a process

---

Education and Sustainable Development in the Context of Crises:
International Case Studies of Transformational Change, 125–139
Copyright © 2025 by Phil Wood. Published by Emerald Publishing Limited.
These works are published under the Creative Commons Attribution (CC BY 4.0) licence. Anyone may reproduce, distribute, translate and create derivative works of these works (for both commercial and non-commercial purposes), subject to full attribution to the original publication and authors. The full terms of this licence may be seen at http://creativecommons.org/licences/by/4.0/legalcode
doi:10.1108/978-1-83797-773-420241008

through which the SDGs can be engaged with at an individual level. This debate is both current and important as it suggests a way in which individual agency can be brought to bear on the global crises we all face.

Keywords: Inner development goals; sustainable development goals; global crises; education; development frameworks

8.1 Introduction

In the summer of 2023, a series of events occurred across the globe: extreme temperatures, wildfires, flooding and the loss of large areas of sea ice, which together add further evidence that the Earth is now exposed to multiple and intensifying crises linked to climate change. The climate crisis has escalated concurrently with a number of other crises, many driven by human activity. For example, the recent global pandemic, the origin of which is uncertain but most likely is the result of intensified interactions between humans and wild animals as the result of resource exploitation (Rulli et al., 2021). There are ongoing weaknesses in the global economy, the hangover of the financial crisis of 2008 (Campello et al., 2010) and the associated rise in economic protectionism and political populism (Ehrlich & Gahagan, 2023). And in addition, there is the continued loss of global biodiversity (Jaureguiberry et al., 2022), and conflicts have further exacerbated international human migration (Erdelen & Richardson, 2020). All of these crises have several characteristics in common, chief among them is the central role played by humans in their emergence. These crises are characterised by extensive tangles of processes, making them both complex and hybrid in character in that human processes are often responsible for intensifying or eroding natural processes. Hence, we can no longer pretend that there are 'firewalls' between human activity and natural world systems, resulting in the ongoing work to declare a new geological epoch, the shift from the Holocene to the Anthropocene, the definition of which is primarily reliant on the appearance of evidence of human activity within the geological record (Lewis & Maslin, 2015).

If we are to continue to increase our understanding of these challenges, as well as learning how to mitigate them, we need to see education as having a pivotal role in developing a positive response. As explained below, 2015 brought the creation of the SDGs, a framework outlining the areas which we need to mitigate against as a process for tackling the multiple crises we face. With only modest impact to date, some argue that the SDGs, while a useful macro-level aide memoire, have achieved little in driving individual behaviour change. This concern for the need to develop individual agency and critical reaction to the crises the global population faces gives a guide to the required direction of travel. Development of the IDGs – a micro-scale framework developed by three Swedish organisations – which focuses on the skills and behaviours individuals will need to foster to support the realisation of macro-level sustainability changes.

In this chapter, we begin by outlining the nature of the systems we are part of and rely on and which are under increasing pressure, triggering the crises we are currently experiencing. We then consider the nature of the issues relating to the SDGs and why they may not support practical change driven by individuals. Finally, we outline the nature of the IDGs and consider their potential importance in meeting the challenges posed by the crises we face, and the crucial role education has in bridging between the micro- and macro-scales to create a coherent process for action and mitigation. In doing so, we argue that IDGs should be at the core of the educational system, in both schools and universities, where they should underpin curriculum creation. While knowledge is important in curricula, it is of little practical use if it cannot be applied to real-world issues by individuals who are confident in working with others to answer hard, ethically complex questions, while also putting emerging ideas into action.

8.2 Humans, Systems and the Nature of Crises

Anthropogenic impact on the environment is not new; humans have altered natural global systems for millennia. Using a transdisciplinary approach sensitive to complex human–environment interactions, Ellis et al. (2013) consider the emergence of human impacts on the biosphere since the start of the Holocene epoch (approximately 10,000 years ago) and show that they have grown and intensified over time, from small, perhaps localised changes accelerating to ever more intense impacts at larger and larger scales,

> The single most important lesson from assessing changes in land use across the Holocene is that changes in the productivity of land-use systems, and especially productivity per area of land, has likely been the main long-term driver of change in human impact on the terrestrial biosphere. (Ellis et al., 2013, p. 8)

As scientists have begun to characterise the plethora of processes and the complexity of associated relationships involved in both human systems and their interaction with the biosphere, they have developed various ways of capturing and exploring this extensive, evolving tangle of processes. Ellis (2015) argues for the development of research which explores what he calls *anthroecological change*, which attempts to track how societies and cultures change and impact on each other and in turn how they interact with the biosphere to bring whole earth system changes. Consequently, studies by Folke et al. (2016) and Donges et al. (2021) exemplify the current development of models which work with the complexity of the interactions across the biotic, societal divide in an attempt to understand the nature of the crises which are now developing at a global level. Donges et al. (2021) model the biophysical subsystem and how it interacts with what they call the socio-metabolic subsystem, that which is at the human–environment interface, and in turn how both of these subsystems interact with the socio-cultural subsystem. This leads to a multi-focal model which begins to track how human and natural systems interact and how such interactions lead to changes in both. As such, we can begin to understand the acute, human-induced crises which face us, leading Folkes et al. (2016) to develop the concept of socio-ecological resilience,

> Social-ecological resilience is the capacity to adapt or transform in the face of change in social-ecological systems, particularly unexpected change, in ways that continue to support human well-being (Chapin et al. 2010, Biggs et al. 2015). (Folkes et al., 2016, p. 42)

Folkes et al. (2016) go on to characterise socio-ecological systems as complex adaptive systems, systems which are open, which interact with other systems and the environment around them, have large numbers of elements which interact in non-linear ways and which are open to feedback loops, especially positive feedback loops which amplify processes or behaviours. Over time, these feedback loops allow the system to change and emerge into new behaviours, hence their characterisation as complex *adaptive* systems. Resilience is therefore the system's capacity to adapt or transform in response to unfamiliar, unexpected events and extreme shocks brought about by the interactions between elements within the system, its interaction with other systems and its wider environment, and the multitude of non-linear processes which interact within its space.

As well as developing an ever greater understanding of complexity and the processes which drive such systems, we also need to develop the traits, abilities and understanding of populations to aid people to work in ways that we have not worked before; an understanding of how human activity is entwined with natural processes, leading to complex interactions, requires us to think very differently, particularly in the parts of the world which have a European philosophical tradition. The required shift in thinking, if not always in action, has already begun to some degree, primarily through the development and adoption by most nations of the SDGs (UN, 2015) as a framework for understanding challenges and adapting to an uncertain future. This shift will be particularly important for the current generation and those to come as they will be responsible, through no fault of their own, for meeting the challenges of the current emerging crises in the future. As D'Angelo (2022, p. 1) states,

> The world is changing rapidly. Globalization, technological innovation, mass displacement, and climate change are shaping the ways in which societies function, progress, or falter. Within this context, children and youth are some of the most affected. Their lives and their futures are on the line—requiring them to develop skills and capacities to cope with the challenges presented in their environments, and to build resilience to the shocks both now and in the future.

In building a sustainability-orientated response among young people, education must play a pivotal role. However, it is a difficult challenge to meet, as many children across the world do not have access to even the most basic schooling. This inequality is beyond the scope of this chapter, but it must be stressed that this is an important issue if populations across the world are to develop positive reactions to the multiple challenges we face. Here, we focus on considering the frameworks which sustainability education should rest on in those nations where universal free education exists.

8.3 The SDGs and Education for Sustainability: Creating a Positive Reaction to Global Crises?

> This Agenda is a plan of action for people, planet and prosperity … All countries and all stakeholders, acting in collaborative partnership, will implement this plan. We are resolved to free the human race from the tyranny of poverty and want and to heal and secure our planet. We are determined to take the bold and transformative steps which are urgently needed to shift the world onto a sustainable and resilient path. As we embark on this collective journey, we pledge that no one will be left behind. (United Nations (UN), 2015, cited in Desai et al. 2018, p. 1)

In 2015, 193 countries became signatories to the UN's 2030 Agenda for sustainable development with explicit aims to end poverty, ensure prosperity for all and to protect the planet. A concrete outcome of this agreement was the creation and adoption of the SDGs (see Fig. 8.1), 17 overarching goals (underwritten by 169 targets) which are the main vehicle for meeting the aims set by the agenda.

They extend from goals relating to the natural world and our interaction with it, for example *Goal 13: Climate Action*, *Goal 14: Life Below Water* and *Goal 15: Life on Land*, to those which focus predominantly on human systems, such as *Goal 1: No Poverty* or *Goal 4: Quality Education*. As such, the goals range across the human–nature continuum and should play a role in understanding and fostering socio-ecological resilience as outlined by Folke et al. (2016) above. The intention of the SDGs is to outline the processes through which human activity will become more sustainable, with fewer pressures on natural earth systems, with a desire to possibly even bolster their health and quality. The goals are intended to be used as overarching principles at country and authority levels, to allow politicians to understand the overall directions of change they have agreed to follow in ameliorating the present crisis position we find ourselves in. Some sectors have

Fig. 8.1. The SDGs. *Source*: UN (n.d.), used under Creative Commons Licence.

started to use the SDGs in a more specific and, sometimes perhaps, unhelpful way. For example, some organisations have started to measure development against them in quite specific ways, one instance being the higher education sector, for example, through the employment of sustainability directors, and asking academics to identify on their web pages which of the SDGs their research is linked to. Pallant et al. (2019) argue that education for sustainable development should act as a vehicle to allow universities to operationalise the SDGs. They focus on the work of the Environmental Science and Sustainability Department at Allegheny College in Meadville, Pennsylvania. A curriculum has been built here to encompass the SDGs, with all students in the department being required to complete five core modules, each of which is infused with elements of the SDGs, as well as basic environment-based skills modules and an optional module focusing on one of five core concepts in the SDGs, namely 'people, prosperity, planet, peace or partnerships' (Pallant et al., 2019, p. 72). The intention here is clear, to inform a strand of education relating to sustainability and the environment, thus making students aware of these issues. In considering the use of the SDGs in the university sector, Steele and Rickards (2021, p. 3) reflect that,

> As the SDG agenda makes clear, universities are a key tool for implementing the SDGs.

Hence, they believe universities should change the way in which they run so that they not only teach about the SDGs but also that they begin to adopt ways of being and thinking that are informed by them.

Thus, the role of education can be argued to be pivotal in developing widescale sustainable responses if populations are to understand the challenges we face. In order to create any meaningful shift in the teaching of sustainability, the interplay between general education, sustainability education (learning about what sustainability is), education for sustainable development (learning about how to ensure a sustainable future), principles in curricula making and action needs to be considered. Unfortunately, much of the education sector remains siloed in its approach to sustainability education, with it often being an add on, a project-based task without knowledge development and a standalone focus without the secure interdisciplinary/transdisciplinary curriculum links which will foster a holistic and critical perspective. Through the lens of sustainability approaches, some schools and universities attempt to adopt the SDGs and try to demonstrate where they are teaching about or addressing them; however, as this was never how they were intended for use, this form of adoption is problematic, as it becomes little more than a label, a signifier that a particular element of a curriculum aligns with a given SDG; at most, the goals become an 'accountancy tool' for deciding on the content to be covered in a programme. Hence, it is difficult to adopt the SDGs within educational settings in anything other than a token fashion, unless there is large-scale buy-in from senior leaders.

In considering how to bring together the SDGs and a more developed sustainability offer in general, it is important to consider the context of learners across educational sectors together with their associated vulnerabilities and inequalities. In this case, it is worth noting that one concern regarding the SGDs is that they are Western centric. This means that they do not fully incorporate the voices and views from the Global South, leading to the potential for exacerbating power imbalances which in time may not reflect learners' backgrounds. To make the teaching of sustainability relevant, it might therefore be argued that changes need to be developed in curricula and programmes which enable learners to see themselves as part of the solution, empowering them to understand and enact change (for a positive example of this, see Nhamo & Mjimba, 2020). But this form of curriculum development is orientated in a different direction to the SDGs, which naturally play a restricted role in highlighting possible content.

One criticism of the SDGs is that they focus on symptoms rather than root causes of unsustainability like overconsumption, injustice and globalisation and avoid challenging the status quo. In order to bring about the transformations needed to address the global crises we are facing, one of the imperatives is ensuring learners understand cause and mitigation fully if they are to effect change. While it is not solely the role of educators to mitigate these shortcomings, there nevertheless needs to be reflection on the approaches used to frame teaching of sustainability whether in primary school or university.

If educators are aware of both the potential utility and limitation of the SDGs and embrace the complexities of engaging with them given their generalist nature, then there is scope for a meaningful education around sustainability to develop. They can be characterised as providing a macro-scale framework that highlights awareness and key themes for discussion within education around sustainability.

Hence, the SDGs, embedded within a sustainability curriculum in both universities and schools, can offer a coherent way of building understanding about the various crises which human populations now face. By understanding the nature of the processes involved, and indeed how they relate to each other as a complex whole, students can begin to develop their understanding including how crises might be averted in the future. However, as outlined above, the SDGs were designed to offer a framework for governments to work towards through national and supranational responses to global crises. This means that there is far less focus on the agency of the individual in how they respond to these goals. There is also the issue that many of the SDGs and the processes on which they are based rely on humans with a mindset focused on making sacrifices to support and encourage environmental sustainability. In contrast, Weintrobe (2021) argues that in general people abide by a psychological mindset of exceptionalism, falsely believing that they are entitled to have whatever they want and that they can rearrange reality to allow themselves to ignore moral and practical limits, in essence because they see themselves in idealised terms. This mindset is the result of the same neoliberal system which has underpinned many of the crises we face as a species, as she states,

> currently it is neoliberal Exceptionalism that is driving mental deregulation and the climate crisis. (Weintrobe, 2021, p. 2)

Thus, we need a framework which directly challenges mindsets and which begins to alter the way individuals perceive the challenges which face them and society as a starting point for developing much-needed skills and traits which will aid in meeting current and future environmental and social challenges. Bendell (2022, p. 17) argues 'it is time for replacing Sustainable Development as the overarching framework for international cooperation with alternative frameworks that are better suited for our new era of increasing crises and disasters', hence the need for a new focus on individual agency to support and augment the macro-scale.

But what should an alternative approach look like? If we go back to the work of Folkes et al. (2016) in the introduction, they identify the idea of a socio-ecological system and from this socio-ecological resilience. As outlined in the introduction, this is based on a realisation, similar to the more amorphous work of post-humanism, that human systems are not divorced from nature but are part of it. Social, economic and cultural systems are all embedded and intimately linked to natural systems. Such a realisation that this is the nature of reality has only emerged in many quarters recently, leading to a slowly dawning acceptance that the planet is in a dire state, and dreams of escaping emerging environmental disaster by leaving the planet for new colonies are really only a pipedream (Latour, 2018). First, it has become ever clearer that the nature of systems is primarily characterised by the multitude of processes which flow and tangle through them. For example, ecosystems regulate, grow and emerge through a multitude of ongoing processes such as photosynthesis, predation, decay and on longer timescale evolution. Second, these processes are complex, as they are non-linear in character, and are open to both negative and positive feedback loops, multitudes of processual interactions and flows, leading to emergence and resulting in new processes, relationships and species. Thus, we are attempting to understand and engage with processually complex adaptive environments and trying to work out how to manage them in sustainable ways. This is a multiscalar (both temporal and spatial) problem, and yet many of our economic, political and educational systems are still ensconced in linear, short-term thinking. We need to develop ways of fusing the micro-scale and the macro-scale in interesting synergies to help individuals understand and engage with these processually complex contexts.

Hence, any reaction to the crises we face needs to consider how it will develop at all of these scales, from the personal to the global. The SDGs give a macro-scale framework, which if used critically might offer the potential for a processually complex understanding of the challenges we face at a micro-scale. But what of the personal level? Here, the wider population needs to understand the nature of the processually complex issues we are facing and at the same time develop the skills and traits which will allow them to work with complex societal issues (IDGs, 2021). Hence, there needs to be a confidence in working within ambiguous contexts, to demonstrate flexibility and creativity and to understand how personal traits and belief systems can impact on the ability to act critically and positively in the world to bring positive and sustainable change. This individual scale of activity is the scale to which the IDGs relate and hence they offer us a way of helping individuals begin to foster the capacities and mindsets they need to meet the crises we face.

8.4 The IDGs – An Agentic Supplement?

The IDGs were initially founded in 2020 by Swedish organisations: the Ekskäret Foundation, The New Division and the 29k Foundation. The work which led to the IDGs grew from initial reflections across these organisations that while we understand many of the large-scale causes of the processes driving the crises we face, material successes in relation to the SDGs have been disappointing. It is identified that this disappointing shift in human activity in the face of mounting processes is the result of a lack of focus on our inner abilities, capacities and skills which are the starting points for tackling these major, global challenges. Hence, if we are to successfully move in a direction which will realise the aims of the SDGs, we first need to foster a set of inner characteristics to enable positive engagement with external, macro-level, aims and goals.

The initial phase of IDG development involved crowdsourcing ideas from practitioners and academics close to sustainability and environmental issues from across the world, working to identify and characterise the qualities and skills central to fostering individuals' ability to engage with and enact positive changes. Initial workshops inviting experts in the field of development were held in 2020, followed by large-scale surveys in 2021, which identified and then ranked items to act as the basis for the final IDG framework (see IDGs, 2021). The result of this process was the framework itself. It is split into five categories of skills and qualities which are argued to be the basis for individuals' ability to engage with the larger developmental issues set out in the SDGs (Table 8.1).

Table 8.1.   The Elements of the IDGs.

Being – relationship to self	• *Inner compass* • *Integrity and authenticity* • *Openness and learning mindset* • *Self-awareness* • *Presence*
Thinking – cognitive skills	• *Critical thinking* • *Complexity awareness* • *Perspective skills* • *Sense-making* • *Long-term orientation and visioning*
Relating – caring for others and the world	• *Appreciation* • *Connectedness* • *Humility* • *Empathy and compassion*
Collaborating – social skills	• *Communication skills* • *Co-creation skills* • *Inclusive mindset and intercultural competence* • *Trust* • *Mobilisation skills*
Acting – driving change	• *Courage* • *Creativity* • *Optimism* • *Perseverance*

Source: Based on IDGs (2021).

The IDG framework thus begins with a consideration of the self, the ways in which we understand and develop our relationships with our own thoughts, feelings and bodies in a way that helps us to act positively when faced with contexts of complexity and ambiguity to create a level of personal resilience through positive reflection and engagement. Next comes the development of our cognitive skills, learning to evaluate information and understanding the world as an interconnected whole, central to enabling us to make wise decisions. Hence, we need to develop skills such as critical perspectives where the focus is on proactively seeking out and understanding contrasting views to generate open mindedness and synthesise alternative insights. At a simple level, this might simply be the understanding that other views to our own exist, while more mature perspective skills allow us to accept that our own views are partial, and therefore incomplete, leading to a more open dialogue with other ideas and an openness to change or the generation of more complex understandings and perspectives. And this leads to a long-term orientation and visioning; where issues are understood as complex and large scale, they cannot be solved quickly. It therefore becomes important that we can think strategically and can understand how current thinking and activity feeds into the long-term horizon for which we are aiming.

But we also need to think beyond ourselves. Here, our ability to relate and care for others becomes crucial with elements such as connectedness, our ability to understand and foster the multitude of connections we have with the greater whole, from our communities and societies to the wider world, both social and natural. It is this sense of connectedness which gives us reasons for caring and being motivated to foster change for the greater whole and offers an ethical motivation to play a role in making the world more sustainable. In our relationships, we also need to demonstrate humility, the ability not to be focused on how we look in a situation but to allow the needs of the situation to dictate how we act. It is related to the idea of not being concerned about our self-image, and hence not feeling the need to project a particular image, but rather focusing on the issue or situation we are dealing with in the most effective way we can and links to empathy and compassion. This is the capacity we have to understand the emotions, views and needs of others and hence how we can relate to them and the wider world in an understanding and positive way, while retaining a sense of self.

The first four of the dimensions in the IDG framework focus on how we relate to ourselves and to others. The fifth then considers how we need to act in bringing change; if we are to make a positive contribution to change in the world, we need to be able to communicate and work with others, often with different views, values and skills to us. This is in sharp contrast to much of the populist politics of the current period and includes co-creation skills, the skills to build and foster collaborative relationships with diverse individuals and groups to co-create in an atmosphere of psychological safety. These together foster spaces for genuine dialogue and collaboration where all feel they have a voice and a stake in the process. This, in turn, leads to the need for an inclusive mindset and intercultural competence, a commitment and ability to seek out and involve a diverse spectrum of individuals who might be interested in the issue of concern, thus ensuring a spectrum of views are expressed and taken account of in decision-making. The ultimate goal is to develop mobilisation skills, by inspiring other people, who sometimes have different views and motivations, to become actively involved in change.

The position advocated by the IDGs has its own criticisms, however. They may be seen as self-indulgent and distracting from tackling concrete problems, as well as being superficial. There is a danger that they are seen as some form of positive psychological intervention which makes individuals feel as if they are doing something worthwhile, while making no or little difference to the world beyond. In addition, the IDGs and SDGs have fundamentally different philosophies and approaches to sustainability, with contrasts regarding inner/outer focus and values. The IDGs are values driven, and therefore, there is a cultural question around implementation in any educational setting as different worldviews might stress different sets of skills and competences. For example, in some communitarian cultures, values might stress the good of the group and expect individuals to foster values and competencies which focus on this collective worldview, as opposed to the generally European individualistic tone of the IDGs as they presently exist.

There is also the ongoing debate about the applicability of what are seen as generalised skills within an educational context of domain-specific disciplines. For some, skills are seen as neither being non-transferable nor generalisable; they only have value and strength within a specific disciplinary context. Here, the argument is that there is no such thing as a thinking skill which can be generically taught and learned and then used in different contexts, as thinking is tethered to knowledge within a given discipline. However, we argue here that such narrow associations might be argued for but are unproven. Instead, we see some skills as having a distance decay effect where those learned in one context will have utility in similar, if different, contexts. Hence, if skills are learned within a physics context, then they will be similar in other scientific contexts and hence still have utility. Some of the other aspects of the framework are more generalisable still as they rely on how we engage with, listen to and involve others. Hence, they have a great potential to be embedded within educational contexts as a medium for fostering personal capacities and skills.

The IDGs framework therefore centres on helping individuals develop a coherent set of skills and competences as a way of facilitating action to engage with and mitigate the crises we face in the 21st century. As such they offer a process which underpins the transitions in mindsets and actions required if individuals are to critically and practically engage with the SDGs.

The importance of education is in providing a meso-scale context for the meeting of the IDGs and the SDGs (Fig. 8.2). The focus of the IDGs aligns well with

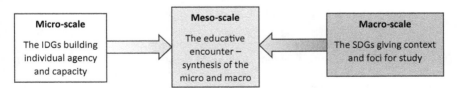

Fig. 8.2. The Role of Education in Bringing Together the Micro-Scale (IDGs) and the Macro-Scale (SDGs). *Source*: Author's own work.

the purpose of education in that they enable learners to explicitly explore the impact of current crises in relation to their own lives, encouraging consideration of their emotions, processes through which they can engage with the issues and demands for actions that they perceive as crucial for developing a more proactive engagement with sustainability. Hence, the IDGs aid the internal changes needed before external change can occur and foster mindsets to engage actively with the macro-scale through the medium of educational activity. This can lead to advocacy for grassroots education and contemplative practices which can serve to mitigate increasing anxieties and a sense of helplessness.

Where sustainability issues are being discussed, the IDGs can add another dimension to the learning experience by making them explicit in discussions about how sustainability can be made to work at different scales. They can also be included in those contexts where ethics are considered and in discussions about well-being and teamwork as aspects of creating positive resilience. In addition, because they are mainly cross-cutting skills and competences, they can be treated as cross-curricula foci, for example, when considering how to work with others and how to handle complex information. Taking the example from above which focused on the Environmental Science and Sustainability Department at Allegheny College in Meadville, Pennsylvania. Pallant et al. (2019, p. 71) highlight that,

> Sterling (2010) who states that an educational focus on critical thinking, capacity building, and resiliency in the face of future uncertainty, threat, and surprise creates individuals who can best respond to the needs of sustainable development efforts.

Hence, in developing their curriculum model, they clearly understand the need to not only look at the content and foci of the SDGs but also to ensure that the educative encounter at the meso-scale pulls in and works with individual agency and capacity.

Paul (2020) discusses the development of environmentally focused 'hackathons' what they call 'Earth Hacks', time-limited events which attempt to develop solutions to real-world problems. The intention of this approach to learning is outlined as following the following philosophy,

> We believe that hackathons can be a powerful tool to advance the Sustainable Development Goals (SDGs) and hope to be able to create a global community of student leaders dedicated to breaking down barriers in tech and applying their skills to solving environmental problems. (Paul, 2020, p. 131)

A hackathon here is an event where students with different skill sets and disciplinary backgrounds come together to produce an innovative solution to a given problem. This format of problem-solving, as the name suggests, originated in software development but has now begun to expand out into other areas including healthcare (D'Ignazio et al., 2016, cited by Paul, 2020) civic issues. Most hackathons finish at the end of the event, but in the case of Earth, Hacks support continues beyond the end of the event to help innovative ideas begin to be realised. Paul describes rich opportunities for individuals to engage with environmental problems in interdisciplinary contexts, so that the focus is on taking creative ideas and turning them into action. This is another example of how education could act as a mesoscale opportunity to explicitly explore individual beliefs, competences and to help in skills development, not only during the hackathon event but over the longer term, hence aiding the development of change action. In this way, hackathons appear to offer huge potential of working towards the SDGs, through individual inner development and collaboration.

8.5 Final Reflections

There is now little doubt that the Earth is being adversely affected by a series of crises which have been triggered and amplified by human activity. These crises are responsible for negative impacts on socio-ecological systems. This is not surprising as scientific evidence has led us to understand the intimate links between the various systems and subsystems which constitute life on the planet. But the major challenge this emerging 'multi-faceted-complex-crisis' creates is how humans are able to react in ways that will lead to positive futures, not only for us but for the health and sustainability of the rest of the biosphere.

The most important reaction that has thus far been developed in an attempt to create a more positive global future is the introduction of the SDGs, an overarching framework intended to direct world leaders in policy generation and development. This is a process to alleviate the impacts of the worst crises facing the planet and in so doing to increase the chance of creating sustainable communities and strengthened natural systems. It is little surprise, therefore, that the SDGs have become a focal point for a wide spectrum of activities and initiatives, including those in education. But their use here needs to be treated with care as the goals were never developed with such detailed uses in mind. There is a clear danger that students will begin to see the goals as remote from both their experiences and their ability to play a positive, meaningful role. In addition, direct interaction with the SDGs ignores the work of those such as Weintrobe (2021) in that they assume that students are already psychologically and emotionally convinced of the need for radical change when in fact they might not be. This means that to make critical and meaningful use of the SDGs in educational settings, there needs to be a view of education as the meso-scale encounter which bridges the personal to the global. It is here that the IDGs can have a major positive impact, helping students gain skills and competences which builds agency, and which open up new ways of being and thinking in relation to the crises which will now define their generation's time on the planet. The framework is not a 'silver bullet', it will not solve the multi-faceted-complex-crisis which young people now face, but it does offer a sound set of individual principles on which they can build and which will play a partial role in heightening the chance that the SDGs will be seen as relevant and attainable.

If we want to change the course of the current climate disaster and lessen and reverse the impacts of the crises faced by our planet, then we need to help the next generation to take action in positive and meaningful ways. Macro-scale destinations are useful to identify; they give us points on the horizon for which we can aim, but in making that journey, it is the character, determination and energy of those who are to make the journey that are of paramount importance, as Pearce (2011) reflects,

> If you want to change the world, first change yourself, then tell others how you did it. Never demand that people change. Inspire them to change using your own change as an example instead.

This might be a positive call to help understand how the IDGs can play a role in helping individuals and communities build the resilience and action they need to create a more positive future.

Acknowledgements

I'd like to acknowledge the help of Dr Aimee Quickfall and Prof Leigh Hoath in giving me feedback on drafts of this chapter. Their insights were invaluable in the development of the arguments laid out here.

References

Bendell, J. (2022). Replacing sustainable development: Potential frameworks for international cooperation in an era of increasing crises and disasters. *Sustainability, 14*(13), 81–85. https://doi.org/10.3390/su14138185

Campello, M., Graham, J. R., & Harvey, C. R. (2010). The long-term cost of the financial crisis. In R. Quail (Ed.), *Lessons from the financial crisis: Causes, consequences, and our economic future* (pp. 571–578). John Wiley & Sons. ISBN: 978-0-470-56177-5.

D'Angelo, S. (2022). Building resilience now and for the future: Adolescent skills to address global challenges. *Development Policy Review, 40*(Suppl. 2), 1–9. https://doi.org/10.1111/dpr.12670

Desai, R. M., Kato, H., Kharas, H., & McArthur, J. W. (Eds.). (2018). *From summits to solutions: Innovations in implementing the sustainable development goals.* Brookings Institution Press. ISBN: 978-0-815-73664-6.

D'Ignazio, C., Hope, A., Metral, A., Brugh, W., Raymond, D., Michelson, B., Achituv, T., & Zuckerman, E. (2016). Towards a feminist Hackathon: The 'Make the Breast Pump Not Suck!' Hackathon. *Digital Journal of Peer Production, 8*.

Donges, J. F., Lucht, W., Cornell, S. E., Heitzig, J., Barfuss, W., Lade, S. J., & Schluter, M. (2021). Taxonomies for structuring models for world-earth systems analysis of the Anthropocene: Subsystems, their interactions and social-ecological feedback loops. *Earth Systems Dynamics, 12*, 1115–1137. https://doi.org/10.5194/esd-12-1115-2021

Ehrlich, S. D., & Gahagan, C. (2023). The multisided threat to free trade: Protectionism and fair trade during increasing populism. *Politics and Governance, 11*(1), 223–236. https://doi.org/10.17645/pag.v11i1.6082

Ellis, E. C. (2015). Ecology in an anthropogenic biosphere. *Ecological Monographs, 85*(3), 287–331. https://doi.org/10.1890/14-2274.1

Ellis, E. C., Kaplan, J. O., Fuller, D. Q., & Verburg, P. H. (2013). Used planet: A global history. *Proceedings of the National Academy of Sciences of the United States of America, 110*(20), 7978–7985. https://doi.org/10.1073/pnas.1217241110

Erdelen, W. R., & Richardson, J. G. (2020). Human migration: Managing its increasing complexity. *Foresight, 22*(1), 109–126. https://doi.org/10.1108/FS-02-2019-0007

Folke, C., Biggs, R., Norström, A. V., Reyers, B., & Rockström, J. (2016). Social-ecological resilience and biosphere-based sustainability science. *Ecology and Society, 21*(3), 41. http://www.jstor.org/stable/26269981

Inner Development Goals. (2021). *Inner development goals: Background, method and the IDG framework*. Retrieved March 21, 2023, from 211201_IDG_Report_Full.pdf (squarespace.com)

Jaureguiberry, P., Titeux, N., Wiemers, M., Bowler, D. E., Coscieme, L., Golden, A. S., Guerra, C. A., Jacob, U., Takahashi, Y., Settele, J., Díaz, S., Molnár, Z., & Purvis, A. (2022). The direct drivers of recent global anthropogenic biodiversity loss. *Science Advances, 8*(45), eabm9982. https://doi.org/10.1126/sciadv.abm9982

Latour, B. (2018). *Down to earth: Politics in the new climatic regime*. John Wiley and Sons Ltd. ISBN: 978-1-509-53057-1.

Lewis, S. L., & Maslin, M. A. (2015). Defining the Anthropocene. *Nature, 519*(7542), 171–180. https://doi.org/10.1038/nature14258

Nhamo, G. & Mjimba, V. (2020). The context: SDGs and institutions of higher education. In G. Nhamo & V. Mjimba (Eds.), *Sustainable development goals and institutions of higher education* (pp. 1–14). Springer Verlag. ISBN: 978-3-030-26157-3.

Pallant, E., Choate, B., & Haywood, B. (2019). How do you teach undergraduate university students to contribute to UN SDGs 2030? In F. W. Leal, A. L. Salvia, R. W. Pretorius, L. L. Brandli, E. Manolas, F. Alves, U. Azeiteiro, J. Rogers, C. Shiel, & P. A. Do (Eds.), *Universities as living labs for sustainable development: Supporting the implementation of the sustainable development goals* (pp. 69–85). Springer International. ISBN: 978-3-030-15604-6.

Paul, S. (2020). University environmental hackathons to further the sustainable development goals. In G. Nhamo & V. Mjimba (Eds.), Sustainable development goals and institutions of higher education (pp. 131–140). Springer Verlag. ISBN: 978-3-030-26157-3.

Pearce, D. (2011). *Single dad laughing: The best of year one*. CreateSpace Independent Publishing Platform. ISBN: 978-1463696160.

Rulli, M. C., D'Odorico, P., Galli, N., & Hayman, D. T. (2021). Land-use change and the livestock revolution increase the risk of zoonotic coronavirus transmission from rhinolophid bats. *Nature Food, 2*(6), 409–416. https://doi.org/10.1038/s43016-021-00285-x

Steele, W., & Rickards, L. (2021). *The sustainable development goals in higher education a transformative agenda?* Palgrave Macmillan. https://doi.org/10.1007/978-3-030-73575-3

Sterling, S. (2010). Learning for resilience, or the resilient learner? Towards a necessary reconciliation in a paradigm of sustainable education. *Environmental Education Research, 1*(5–6), 511–528. https://doi.org/10.1080/13504622.2010.505427

UN. (2015). *General assembly, transforming our world: The 2030 agenda for sustainable development*. A/70/1. https://sustainabledevelopment.un.org/content/documents/21252030%20Agenda%20for%20Sustainable%20Development%20web.pdf?ref=truth11.com

UN. (n.d.). *Sustainable development goals kick off with start of new year*. https://www.un.org/sustainabledevelopment/blog/2015/12/sustainable-development-goals-kick-off-with-start-of-new-year/#

Weintrobe, S. (2021). *Psychological roots of the climate crisis. Neoliberal exceptionalism and the culture of uncare*. Bloomsbury. ISBN: 9781501372865.

Chapter 9

Conclusion

Miriam Sang-Ah Park

Nottingham Trent University, UK

Abstract

This concluding chapter summarises and discusses some of the key messages from the chapters in this book. Careful consideration of the terms introduced, defined and refined in this book (e.g., crises) is made, along with the contexts in which such refined definitions may be especially useful for research, scholarship and practice in higher education. The points of intersections among this book's chapters and the authors' arguments are also highlighted in this chapter.

Keywords: Education; international; sustainable development; crises; glocal; global

This edited volume set out to explore and discuss education and international sustainable development in the context of crises. The most significant points the contributing authors have raised relate to the strong connection and synergetic impact that the collaboration between education and international sustainable development can create and the diverse ways in which 'crises' can be defined and experienced across different educational and cultural contexts. All the chapters highlight the importance of contextualisation of education and, in particular, raising awareness for sustainable development, in order to better prepare students for the present as well as future crises. In this final chapter, I will revisit some of the unique messages from individual chapters as well as discuss some common themes that recur despite the diversity of the contexts.

Education and Sustainable Development in the Context of Crises:
International Case Studies of Transformational Change, 141–144
Copyright © 2025 by Miriam Sang-Ah Park. Published by Emerald Publishing Limited. These works are published under the Creative Commons Attribution (CC BY 4.0) licence. Anyone may reproduce, distribute, translate and create derivative works of these works (for both commercial and non-commercial purposes), subject to full attribution to the original publication and authors. The full terms of this licence may be seen at http://creativecommons.org/licences/by/4.0/legalcode
doi:10.1108/978-1-83797-773-420241009

As Boin et al. (2020) have claimed, a crisis leads to a disruption in the normal operations, and we saw education having to deal with such crises during the pandemic in the recent years. Student expectations, delivery of teaching and assessment modes were only the most obvious of the changes that came with the pandemic, meaning that through this period, significant efforts to maintain academic standards and quality were observed. Furthermore, there were plenty of other socio-political events that occurred during and following the pandemic – such as the war in Ukraine and Gaza and instances of extreme weather events fuelled by climate change that exerted combined pressure on education institutions and educators.

As the authors of Chapter 2 call to our attention, quality education is one of the 17 United Nations' (UN) sustainable development goals (SDGs), and this goal carries much weight in the sense that it intersects with other SDGs such as reduced inequality, sustainable cities and communities, good health and well-being and many more. While there is a universal drive towards improving education, the challenges in regions with social and political instabilities are apparent (Agbedahin, 2019). Along with Chapter 2, all other chapters in this book outlined some of these challenges and also presented current projects as well as potential future solutions to tackling these challenges.

Importantly, this book also presented how higher education institutions outside of the typical so-called WEIRD – that is Western, Educated, Industrialised, Rich and Democratic – countries coped with and adapted to the changes and challenges of these years. For s some of the challenges that an international campus faces and the need for a better intercultural communication in Iraq. Working at an American institution within Iraq (the American University of Iraq Sulaimani), staff reported challenges posed by both the differences in cultural values and communication style in trying to deliver and manage effective education to students enrolled in such an institution. At the same time, however, the authors demonstrated how scholars at this international campus were actively promoting sustainable goals, especially by raising awareness, instigating policy discussions and building capacity with regard to their students and teachers.

Similarly, we read about school leadership in Somalia in the midst of the armed conflict that has affected the country and schools in Chapter 4. The authors present critical insights and research findings on primary school headteachers' experience through the challenging times. While the external, uncontrollable crises posed significant difficulties, headteachers' skills and resilience helped reduce some of their impact and led to better education for the students. The authors also suggest efficacy and especially collective efficacy (e.g., DeWitt, 2017) as a potential adaptive mechanism that can help improve school climate. This idea echoes Capone et al. (2019) who found collective efficacy to help reduce burden and stress in schoolteachers.

Chapter 6 discusses migration as one of the key themes of the UN SDGs and the need for higher education to consider both the reasons for migration and its implications for education. With globalisation and especially the crises one faces in their culture of origin, we see a huge amount of migration happening around the globe, and this suggests that higher education institutions need to understand the trends and changes and adapt flexibly and openly to identify opportunities as well for educators and students alike, which the authors highlight as an important step towards sustainable development.

Chapter 7 highlights the need to expand and improve education for global citizenship. In facing the global crises and the uncertainties that accompany these crises, students can be better prepared if education helped them to form a clearer sense of identity and agency. The author suggests that the contextualisation of communicative acts and, in particular, the introduction of so-called learning lifeworlds can help achieve this goal, finding her methods to have worked well with a group of students in Hong Kong.

Chapter 8 discusses the important interplay between the macro-level, external goals (as listed in UN SDGs), and the micro-level, internal goals (Inner Development Goals or individual actor's own setting of and capacity building towards goals). The author argues that it is a better idea to start from the individual to effect these goals if one realises that the systems are built upon individuals' perceptions, beliefs and actual behaviours, and that this would lead to better outcomes in tackling the global challenges.

Our book has raised an important point about the role of higher education in today's fast-changing world. For instance, Chapters 3 and 5 concur in that the objective of international higher education in times of crisis should be to train students to be community leaders as well as agents of change. The authors argue that higher education institutions carry the responsibility to equip the next generation to be fully aware of the local and global issues, to be independent thinkers so that they have the capacity to tackle the crises that affect themselves and their local community and be able to lead on solutions.

This book has appealed to be an interesting concept of glocalism, which combines the processes of localisation and globalisation. As is pointed out in Chapter 2, it is recognised that the locality and the crises it faces often mirror those of the global world, and also that in today's world, both are closely intertwined with one another. This recognition that global and local issues are closely interconnected, thus giving shape to crises in specific ways across different contexts, also highlights the need for international education and its contribution towards sustainable development.

The COVID-19 pandemic was such an example in which the crises higher education institutions faced affected the global world (e.g., mode of teaching had to be transformed according to the lockdown rules). These crises also hit local regions in ways that were more specific (e.g., in South Korea, this led to a further polarisation of resources dividing the capital city region from the rest of the country). The authors' suggestion for tackling these issues in Chapter 5 was to educate and empower university students in such a way that they embrace sustainable development both regionally and globally.

Across the chapters, there is a unanimous message that we need to pay more attention to the interconnectedness among the concepts, actors and levels of agents that may seem disparate and loosely related. The best way to tackle the 'crises' may be that we recognise the role of education in raising awareness, training and empowering the young generation so that they can be active agents of international sustainable development. In this book, we have seen discussions that connect the global and the local issues and how they impact on the glocal community. We have also witnessed both the divisions between and the interplay of impact originating from the external circumstances, the systems and the actors, as well as regions and countries coming together and having a bigger influence on one another in today's world of globalisation and resulting international mobility. This book has highlighted the importance of re-thinking education across various policy levels and countries, recognising its role in training people to be able to manage and survive various crises in the present as well as the future. Another important message from this book, leading from all of these conclusions, may be that, as self-determination theory (Deci & Ryan, 2012) and the Inner Development Goals (2021) suggest, we focus on building resilience by way of increasing the sense of agency, developing the internal strength and capacity that prepares one against the external challenges. Finally, we see that a clear identity, for both education institution and students, is what will foster their resilience and adaptability.

References

Agbedahin, A. V. (2019). Sustainable development, education for sustainable development, and the 2030 agenda for sustainable development: Emergence, efficacy, eminence, and future. *Sustainable Development, 27*(4), 669–680. https://doi.org/10.1002/sd.1931

Boin, A., Ekengren, M., & Rhinard, M. (2020). Hiding in plain sight: Conceptualizing the creeping crisis. *Risk, Hazards & Crisis in Public Policy, 11*(2), 116–138. https://doi.org/10.1002/rhc3.12193

Capone, V., Joshanloo, M., & Park, M. S. A. (2019). Burnout, depression, efficacy beliefs, and work-related variables among school teachers. *International Journal of Educational Research, 95*, 97–108. https://doi.org/10.1016/j.ijer.2019.02.001

Deci, E. L., & Ryan, R. M. (2012). Self-determination theory. In *Handbook of theories of social psychology* (Vol. 1(20), pp. 416–436). Sage. ISBN 9781446269008.

DeWitt, P. M. (2017). *School climate: Leading with collaborative efficacy.* Corwin.

Inner Development Goals. (2021). Inner development goals: Background, method and the IDG framework. Retrieved March 21, 2023, from 211201_IDG_Report_Full.pdf (squarespace.com)

Index

Acculturation of international students, 97
Agenda for Sustainable Development (2030), 77
American University of Iraq, Sulaimani (AUIS), 27–29, 35–36, 39
  organisational affiliates of, 33–35
American-style liberal arts universities, 26
American-style university model, 26, 28
Anthroecological change, 127
APP, 35
Approaches to learning skills (ATL skills), 117
AUIS Center for Archaeology and Cultural Heritage (CACHE), 38
AUIS Entrepreneurship and Innovation Centre (AEIC), 33, 35
Average citation per year (ACPY), 85

Benadir regional administration, 46–47
Bibliometric analysis, 75
Bibliometric methodology, 79–80
Biophysical subsystem, 127
Brain drain phenomenon, 76
Brain gain, 76, 97
BREXIT referendum (2016), 14
Brundtland Report of the United Nations, 77

Capability approach, 4
Capital accumulation in education mobility, 97–98

Carbon Neutral ESG Sharing Forum (2030), 62
Cascading crises, 15
Center for Gender and Development Studies (CGDS), 29, 33, 36, 38
Central government of South Korea, 59
Chung-Ang University, 62
Citation analysis, 85, 99
Citizenship education, 110–111, 115
Climate change, 13
  disasters, 16
Cluster analysis, 81, 92
Co-authorship analysis, 89
Co-creation skills, 134
Collaboration trends in migration studies in education, 85–91
Collective identity, 113
Colonisation, 119
Communication challenges, 35–36
Communicative action to address gap in educating for global citizenship, Habermas' theory of, 112–115
Communicative reality, 112
Community betterment, individual and personal efforts for, 38
Community mobilization, 48
Conflict-affected environment, school leadership in, 48–50
Connectedness, 134
COVID-19
  and impact on higher education institutions in South Korea, 61
  pandemic, 11, 143
Creeping crises, 10–11
Crises, 5, 10–12, 49, 141

education in International
    sustainable development
    in ever-existing context of,
    15–16
  glocalisation and, 12–14
  around world and impact on
    sustainable development,
    14–15
Crisis, 10, 12, 58
Critical thinking skills, 26, 28,
    30, 35
Crucial capital, 97
Cuban missile crisis (1962), 12
Cultural adaptation in higher
    education, 97
Culture, 113
Curriculum model, 136

Data collection, 50
Data sorting, 50
Descriptive indicators, 82
Digital education, 16
Disability, 33
Disadvantaged students, 63
Disaster, 10–11
Disclosure of ESG information by
    universities, 64
Discourse of international student
    mobility, 94–95
Dissemination of ESG information
    by universities, 64
Diversity, 31, 84, 94
Dual-level impact, 31
Dynamic relationship, 93

Earth Hacks, 136
Earthquake, 12
East Africa, 5, 13, 15
Economic crises, 5
Economic crisis, 14–15
Ecosystems, 132
Education, 3–4, 16, 93, 141
  capital accumulation in education
    mobility, 97–98

characteristics of migration studies
    in, 82–85
collaboration trends in migration
    studies in, 85–91
conceptual structure of migration
    studies in, 91–93
for global citizenship,
    110–112, 117
institutions, 61
in international sustainable
    development in ever-
    existing context of crises,
    15–16
migration in, 75–76
sector, 130
for sustainability, 129–132
Education for sustainable development
    (ESD), 4, 59, 61
Education Sector Strategic Plan
    (ESSP), 46, 49
Educational migration, 78
  for sustainable development, 77–78
Educational mobility, regional
    dynamics and neo-
    nationalism in, 95–96
Educational research, 75
Educational systems, 76
Educators, 131
Ego-identity, 113
Ekskäret Foundation, 132
Emergency, 10–12
Employability, 78, 89, 97
Enormity, 52
Environment, society, and
    governance (ESG), 59
  committees, 62
  disclosure and dissemination
    of ESG information by
    universities, 64
  management of universities, 63
  operation of ESG committee and
    efforts to spread ESG
    culture, 63
University Cluster, 64

University Cluster Agreement Ceremony and Forum (2023), 64
European debt crisis, The, 14
European Union (EU), 13
Exclusion criteria, 79
Exploratory factor analysis, 82

Forced migration, 76

Global citizenship, 4
　education, 110–112
　Habermas' theory of communicative action to address gap in educating for, 112–115
Global contexts, 5
Global crises, 143
　positive reaction to, 129
Global South, 131
Global world, 143
Globalization, 18, 128
Glocal community, 144
Glocalisation, 5, 10, 15
　and crises, 12–14
Glocalism concept, 143

'Habermas' assertion, 120
'Habermas' theory of communicative action, 110, 116, 120–121
　to address gap in educating for global citizenship, 112–115
Habermasian theory, 120
Hackathons, 136
Headteachers, 50, 53
　in private schools, 48
Higher education
　change in participation and perception, 65–67
　context, 58
　COVID-19 and impact on higher education institutions in South Korea, 61
　cultural adaptation and internationalisation in, 97
　historical background, 60–61
　in post-conflict settings, 30
　regional cooperations between universities and local government, 65
　SDGs and ESG management, 61–64
　in South Korea, 60
　systems, 26, 30
Higher education institutions (HEIs), 30, 58, 94, 99, 142
Human capital development, 95
Human capital model, 94
Human systems, 129
　and nature of crises, 127–128
Hurricane, 12

Incheon Port Corporation, 65
Incheon Transportation Corporation, 65
Incheon University LINC 3.0 Project Group, 65
Inclusion criteria, 79
Inconsistent strategies, 36–37
Individual engagement and development, 31
Industrialisation, 58
Inner development goals (IDG), 126, 132–137, 144
　development, 133
　framework, 134–135
　humans, systems and nature of crises, 127–128
　SDGs and education for sustainability, 129–132
Innovation, 128
Institute of Regional and International Studies (IRIS), 29, 33
Institutional Review Board, The, 33
Intercultural competence, 134
International Baccalaureate Diploma Programmes (IBDP), 116

International Baccalaureate Middle Years Programmes (IBMYP), 116–117
International Baccalaureate Organisation (IBO), 111
International Baccalaureate Primary Years Programmes (IBPYP), 116
International development, 5
International educational mobility, 97
International migration, 75, 98
International Organization for Migration (IOM), 74
International schools, 111
International student mobility, 95
  discourse and politics of, 94–95
  factors shaping, 96–97
International students, 78
  motivational factors for, 98
International study, trans/national academic mobilities and, 95
International sustainable development, 5, 16, 141
  education in international sustainable development in ever-existing context of crises, 15–16
Internationalisation in higher education, 97

Japanese Colonial Period, 60
Jeonju-University ESG Agreement, 65

Kangwon National University, 66
Konkuk University, 62
Korea University's Social Contribution Centre, 63
Korean higher education institutions, 63
Korean sustainable development goals (K-SDGs), 61
Korean War, 60
Kurdish community's hesitancy to accept liberal values, 38
Kurdish/Arab community, 37

Leadership
  conceptualising, 47–48
  development, 49
Learning lifeworlds, 143
Liberal arts curriculum, 26, 28
Liberal values, Kurdish community's hesitancy to accept, 38
Lifelong learning, 74, 77–78
Limited funding, 37
Local contexts, 5
Local government, regional cooperations between universities and, 65

Macro-scale destinations, 138
Marginalised communities, 36
Metropolitan Landfill Management Corporation, 65
Microcategorisation approach, 83
Migration, 74–75, 93
  analysis of identified data sources, 80–82
  capital accumulation in education mobility, 97–98
  characteristics of migration studies in education, 82–85
  collaboration trends in migration studies in education, 85–91
  conceptual considerations and literature review, 75
  conceptual structure of migration studies in education, 91–93
  cultural adaptation and internationalisation in higher education, 97
  discourse and politics of international student mobility, 94–95
  in education, 75–76
  educational migration for sustainable development, 77–78
  factors shaping international student mobility, 96–97

Index 149

identification of scholarly sources, 79
implications and future directions, 99
methodological considerations, 78
motivational factors for international students, 98
regional dynamics and neo-nationalism in educational mobility, 95–96
research design, 78
results, 82
trans/national academic mobilities and international study, 95
Military conflicts, 27
Militia group, 52
Millennium development goals (MDGs), 77
Ministry of Education (MoE), 58–59
in South Korea, 60
Ministry of Trade, Industry and Energy (MTIE), 64
Mixed-methods approach, 116
Multi-faceted-complex-crisis, 137
Multidimensional crises, 13

National academic mobilities and international study, 95
National school systems, 111
Natural disasters, 5
Neo-nationalism in educational mobility, 95–96
Neo-racism, 95
New Division, The, 132
Non-governmental organisations (NGOs), 29, 50

Onyx's conceptualisation of impact, 31
Onyx's model of social impact, 31
Organisation for Economic Co-operation and Development (OECD), 76, 112
Organisational affiliates of AUIS, 33–35

Participants, 53
Personal identity, 113
Place, Problem, and Project method (P3L method), 59
Policy landscape of Somali Private Education System
Benadir regional administration, 46–47
conceptualising leadership, 47–48
findings, 50–52
methodology, 50
recommendations, 53
school leadership in conflict-affected environment, 48–50
Political crises, 5
Political socialization, 30
Politics of international student mobility, 94–95
Population decline, 67
Positive feedback loops, 128
Post-2015 migration crises in Europe, 15
Post–conflict society, 26–27
Presidential Committee on Ageing Society and Population Policy (PCASPP), 58
Private schools in Mogadishu, 48
Problem based learning (PBL), 59
Programme for International Student Assessment (PISA), 89
Push–pull theory of international students, 98

Qualitative analysis, 32
Qualitative data, 116
Quality education, 15, 142

Reflexive thematic analysis, 117
Refugee education, 89
Regional cooperations between universities and local government, 65
Regional dynamics, 96
in educational mobility, 95–96

Regional Innovation Scheme project (RIS project), 59, 66
Regular crises, 10
Research questions (RQs), 78
Resilience, 128
Russia-Ukraine war, 10

Scholarly collaborations, 85
School cultures, 113
School leadership
  in conflict-affected environment, 48–50
  in Somalia, 142
School-age population, 59
Self-determination theory, 144
Self-efficacy concept, 65
Self-replicating phenomenon, 114
Self-sustaining phenomenon, 114
Semi-structured interviews, 32
Seoul National University, 64
Social capital, 66–67, 76, 97
Social cohesion, 28, 77
Social impact of American Liberal Arts University
  AUIS, 28–29
  communication challenges, 35–36
  conceptual framework, 31–32
  findings, 35
  individual and personal efforts for community betterment, 38
  Kurdish community's hesitancy to accept liberal values, 38–39
  limited funding, 37
  literature review, 29–30
  methodology, 32–33
  organisational affiliates of AUIS, 33–35
  unclear institutional vision and inconsistent strategies, 36–37
Social justice, 87, 89, 94
Social role of universities, 29–30
Social-ecological resilience, 128
Socially responsible investing (SRI), 63
Society, 113

Socio-ecological systems, 128
Socio-metabolic subsystem, 127
Somali private schools, 46
Somalia, 6, 46
  education system, 53
  Somalia-related studies, 49
South Korea, 58
  higher education in, 60–67
Spiritual competency, 52
Staff faced repercussions, 52
Student self-directedness and independence, 117–118
  impact of lifeworld on, 117
Students Club Research Projects, 66
Supply chain management (SCM), 62
Sustainability, 95
  education for, 129–132
  issues, 136
  sustainability-orientated response, 128
Sustainable development, 59, 75, 131
  educational migration for, 77–78
  recent crises around world and impact on, 14–15
Sustainable development goals (SDGs), 5, 15, 59, 74, 110, 126, 136, 142 (*see also* Inner development goals (IDG))
  and education for sustainability, 129–132
  management, 61–64
Swedish organizations, 132
System colonization, withstanding threat of, 118–120

Takween (business accelerator), 34, 37
Teacher–student communicative action
  education for global citizenship, 110–112
  Habermas' theory of communicative action to address gap in educating, 112–115

impact of lifeworld on student self-directedness and independence, 117
methodology, 115–117
student self-directedness and independence, 117–118
withstanding threat of system colonization, 118–120
Thematic data analysis, 33
Theorisation, 4
Total citation (TC), 85
Trans/national academic mobilities and international study, 95
Transdisciplinary approach, 127
Trumpism, 5
29k Foundation, the, 132

UNAI KOREA, 65
Unclear institutional vision, 36–37
UNESCO Institute for Lifelong Learning (UIL), 77
UNICEF, 50
Unintended impacts, 27
United Nations (UN), 77
  Agenda (2030), 77
  Millennium Summit, 77
United Nations Development Programme (UNDP), 77
  Human Development Report, 4

United Nations Educational, Scientific and Cultural Organization (UNESCO), 50, 75
University, 31, 58
  disclosure and dissemination of ESG information by, 64
  regional cooperations between local government and, 65
  social role of, 29–30
University of Michigan, The, 31

Validity claims, 113
Volatile, uncertain, complex and ambiguous world (VUCA world), 120

Web of Science (WOS), 75, 83
Western, Educated, Industrialised, Rich and Democratic countries (WEIRD countries), 142
World Bank, 50
World Commission on Environment and Development (WCED), 77
World War II (WWII), 5

Yonsei University, 64